797,885 Books
are available to read at

www.ForgottenBooks.com

Forgotten Books' App
Available for mobile, tablet & eReader

ISBN 978-1-334-43201-9
PIBN 10734048

This book is a reproduction of an important historical work. Forgotten Books uses state-of-the-art technology to digitally reconstruct the work, preserving the original format whilst repairing imperfections present in the aged copy. In rare cases, an imperfection in the original, such as a blemish or missing page, may be replicated in our edition. We do, however, repair the vast majority of imperfections successfully; any imperfections that remain are intentionally left to preserve the state of such historical works.

Forgotten Books is a registered trademark of FB &c Ltd.
Copyright © 2017 FB &c Ltd.
FB &c Ltd, Dalton House, 60 Windsor Avenue, London, SW19 2RR.
Company number 08720141. Registered in England and Wales.

For support please visit www.forgottenbooks.com

1 MONTH OF FREE READING

at

www.ForgottenBooks.com

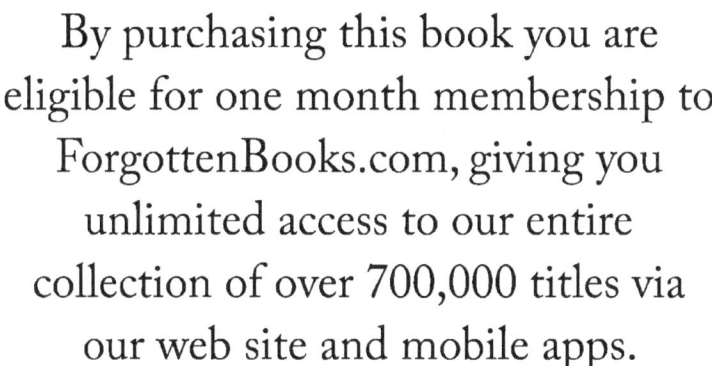

By purchasing this book you are eligible for one month membership to ForgottenBooks.com, giving you unlimited access to our entire collection of over 700,000 titles via our web site and mobile apps.

To claim your free month visit:

www.forgottenbooks.com/free734048

* Offer is valid for 45 days from date of purchase. Terms and conditions apply.

English
Français
Deutsche
Italiano
Español
Português

www.forgottenbooks.com

Mythology Photography **Fiction**
Fishing Christianity **Art** Cooking
Essays Buddhism Freemasonry
Medicine **Biology** Music **Ancient Egypt** Evolution Carpentry Physics
Dance Geology **Mathematics** Fitness
Shakespeare **Folklore** Yoga Marketing
Confidence Immortality Biographies
Poetry **Psychology** Witchcraft
Electronics Chemistry History **Law**
Accounting **Philosophy** Anthropology
Alchemy Drama Quantum Mechanics
Atheism Sexual Health **Ancient History**
Entrepreneurship Languages Sport
Paleontology Needlework Islam
Metaphysics Investment Archaeology
Parenting Statistics Criminology
Motivational

AN ESSAY

ON THE

POWER and HARMONY

OF

PROSAIC NUMBERS:

Being a SEQUEL to one on the

POWER of NUMBERS

And the

PRINCIPLES of HARMONY

IN

POETIC COMPOSITIONS.

LONDON:

Printed by JAMES WAUGH, for M. COOPER, at the Globe in Pater-noster Row. MDCCXLIX.

Engl.
Noble
9.9.27
15471

820.56
N4

PREFACE.

THE following Essay is chiefly intended for the Benefit of those, whose Province calls them to employ much of their Time and Study in Composition; and to engage their Attention to one Branch of that Art, which though cultivated with great Assiduity and Exactness by the Antients, is but little known to many, and much neglected by most of the Moderns.

What I mean, is a critical Regard to the Structure of their Periods; or such a Care in the Choice and Disposition of their Words as will give them that agreeable Flow which the Antients called *Rhythmus:* The Harmony of which every good Ear perceives, but the Principles from whence it flows, the Rules on which it depends, and the Way to acquire it, very few have any Knowledge of or Concern about.

And it is really somewhat surprising that our modern Rhetoricians should lay so little Stress upon a Thing which the antient Orators considered as so important. The true Reason of which I believe is this, it is generally looked upon as one of those Minutenesses of Stile which are below the Notice of an elevated Genius, or at least would be too dull and dry a Study to be relished by Persons of a refined Taste; and so the whole Business is left to the Ear, by which the Writer is led, and the Reader judges, at Random. But to this Case is applicable that well known and just Observation, *Ea parva non ducenda sunt, sine quibus magna consistere non possunt.* Those Things are not to be counted little or unnecessary, without which great Things can never be attained. Otherwise the Elements of all Languages and the Rudiments of all Sciences may be counted low and trifling.

It

It is the Connection which thefe Things have with greater, that gives them their Importance, and a Claim to our Attention. Which is all the Apology I fhall make for any Thing which may be thought minute or dry in the following Effay.

But however dull or difficult fuch a Study may appear to the Reader at firft, I am well fatisfied, that as foon as he comes to make a little Progrefs in it, he will be fully convinced that the Pleafure and Importance of it are more than equal to all the Pains he took to attain it. And of this let one who is very well verfed in this Subject be Judge.------" Many Writers (fais
" he) both in Verfe and Profe, have been
" very exact in their Choice of Words, e-
" legant and adapted to the Subject; but
" being deftitute of a juft Ear, run into
" diffonant and jarring Meafures, by which
" they lofe their Labour and fpoil the
" whole. Their Productions are unplea-
" fant and naufeous to the Reader. Others,
" though fo unlucky as to chufe mean and
" vulgar Words, yet by arranging them in a
" melodious Manner, have given a furpri-
" fing Beauty to their Diction. The
" Truth

" 'Truth is, the Pofition of Words feems
" to bear the fame Proportion to the Choice
' of them, as the Words themfelves have
" to the Sentiments. As the fineft Senti-
" ment is cold and languid when not clo-
" thed with the Ornament of beautiful
" Language, fo the Invention of the moft
" pure and elegant Expreffions will have
' fmall Effect unlefs you add an harmo-
" nious Compofition (*a*)."

" It would be too dull a Piece of Cri-
" ticifm (as the fame Author obferves) for
" the Generality of Readers to confider
" the Nature, Formation and Sound of the
" different Vowels, their Junction with
" Confonants, and the Formation of Syl-
" lables; the due Length and Shortnefs
" of thefe, and what Pronunciation is pro-
" per to them; and to define their Num-
" bers would appear Scholaftic, and down-
" right Pedantry to a Modern, who loves
" his Eafe too much to be fettered by fuch
" Rules. But this is certain that he who
" is wholly unexperienced in a Theory of
" this Kind, and never took the Trouble
" to reflect on it, cannot poffibly be Maf-
" ter

(*a*) See *Geddes* on the Compofition of the Antients, p. 3.

" ter of a beautiful Stile: he writes at ran-
" dom, is guided by no Rule in his Com-
" pofition, and knows nothing of the juft
" Meafures and Cadency of Language (*b*)."
――― And again, " What ever renders a Pe-
" riod fweet and pleafant, makes it alfo
" graceful; a good Ear is the Gift of Na-
" ture; it may be much improved but not
" acquired by Art. Who ever is poffeffed
" of it, will fcarcely need dry critical Pre-
" cepts to enable him to judge of a true
" Rhythmus, and Melody of Compofition:
" Juft Numbers, accurate Proportions, a
" mufical Symphony, magnificent Figures,
" and that Decorum which is the Refult
" of all thefe, are *Unifon* to the human
" Mind; we are fo framed by Nature that
" their Charm is irrefiftable (*c*)."

In this then the Ear is a better Judge than Guide; it will much eafier determine what a true Rhythmus is (*d*), than teach us how to attain it. But as *Tully* fome-

where

(*b*) Id. p. 18, 26.
(*c*) Id. p. 10, 11.
(*d*) Et tamen omnium longitudinum at brevitatum in fonis, ficut acutarum graviumque vocum, Judicium ipfa natura in auribus noftris collocavit.――― Aures enim, vel animus aurium Nuntio, naturalem quandam in fe continet vocum omnium Menfionem. *Cic.* Orator §. 51, 53.

where tells us that the Laws of Verse were originally invented, by reflecting upon and attending to that Order and Position of Words and Quantities which were most pleasing to the Ear, so all the Rules for attaining a true Rhythm in Prose Compositions have the same Original. And by considering what it is that the Ear most approves, Laws are invented and Rules contrived for acquiring such a Stile in writing, which at once conveys Pleasure to the Ear and Improvement to the Mind; by which we are to judge of all Composition in general, whether of Verse or Prose.

And here let it be observed, that as the Ear confirms those Rules which lead us to a perfect Rhythm, so the Rules will be some Help to the Ear in judging of it.

I shall only add, that the following Piece pretends to nothing more than its Title expresses, *viz.* an *Essay* on the Subject. To have gone deeper into it would not have consisted with a proper Application to another Kind of Studies, to which the Providence of God more immediately calls me. If it be a Means of exciting
others

others to purſue it further, or may be helpful to any young Lovers of Learning, and eſpecially the Students and Candidates for the ſacred Miniſtry, to facilitate their Compoſitions, and give an eaſy Grace and Dignity to their Language, I apprehend it may be of ſome Service to Mankind; which is all the End I aim at.

THE
CONTENTS.

CHAP. I.

THE high Esteem the Antients had for numerous Composition. The general Neglect of it among the Moderns. The Reasons of that Neglect. And the Weakness of those Reasons.
Page 1,—9.

CHAP. II.

The Nature and Quality of simple Numbers or Feet separately considered.
p. 9,—17.

CHAP.

CHAP. III.

The different Disposition or Combination of the Numbers, is that which constitutes the Difference between a smooth and a rough Stile. p. 17,—21.

CHAP. IV.

The Manner of reducing Prosaic Numbers, or of examining the Feet of which any Period is composed. p. 21,—27.

CHAP. V.

Concerning the most proper Feet to close a Sentence. p. 27,—33.

CHAP. VI.

Of Poetic Prose. p. 33,—38.

CHAP. VII.

Of Prosaic Poetry. p. 38,—48.

CHAP. VIII.

The Composition of some of our best English Writers considered with Regard to their Numbers. p. 48,—61.

CHAP.

CHAP. IX.

Rules proper to be observed in Order to acquire a numerous Stile. p. 61,—72.

CHAP. X.

The Advantage of a numerous Composition. p. 72,—76.

AN ESSAY ON THE Power of Numbers, &c.

CHAP. I.

INTRODUCTION.

The high Esteem the Antients had for numerous Composition. The general Neglect of it among the Moderns. The Reasons of that Neglect. And the Weakness of those Reasons.

NUMEROUS Composition was held in great Esteem among the best antient Writers, especially about the Time of *Cicero*.

Isocrates, who is universally admired for his Numbers, observing the Effect which they had upon the Mind in Verse, is said to be the first that introduced them into Profe; which he probably effected by reducing them to Rules, and by obferving thofe Rules in his Profaic Compofitions.

But *Cicero* attributes the Invention of them partly to *Thrafymachus*, who was before *Ifocrates*, aud partly to *Gorgias*, who was his Cotemporary but Senior; who were both exceffively fond of this Ornament of Stile, as Men generally are of their own Difcoveries; and fais, that *Ifocrates* only improved upon their Thoughts, moderated the Numbers of which they were fo lavifh, and reduced that Kind of Writing to its proper Standard (*a*).

The Invention of this Art then is an Honour for certain due to the *Greeks*; " and it does not appear to have been obferved by the *Romans* till near the Time of *Tully*. And even then it was by no Means univerfally received: the antient and lefs numerous Manner of Compofition had ftill many Admirers, who were fuch *Enthufiafts to Antiquity* as to adopt their very Defects (*b*)."

However it foon made its Way among them; and *Cicero* obferves, That in his Time Profe had its meafured Cadence as well as Verfe (*c*); and the effential Difference between them was no longer that which is contained in the old Definition of *foluta et ftricta Oratio*, or that the one was confined to Meafures and the other left at Liberty, but that the Meafures in Profe were more loofe and various than thofe in Verfe.

Nor

(*a*) Cic. Orat. Ed. Lond. Tom. 1. p. 165. b.
(*b*) Fitzofborn's Letters. Let. 24.
(*c*) Nam etiam Poetæ Quæftionem attulerunt, Quidnam effet illud quo ipfi differunt ab Oratoribus; Numero videbantur antea maximè et verfu: nunc apud Oratores jam ipfe numerus increbuit. Cic. in Oratore.

[3]

Nor did that great Orator himſelf think this Art beneath his Notice. He wrote upon it, and very happily ſerved himſelf of it. By the Power of Numbers united with that of Reaſon, he confounded the audacious *Cataline*, and ſilenced the eloquent *Hortenſius*. His perſwaſive Art would have loſt its Force without the Help of the *Rhythmus*, and all *Demoſthenes's Thunder* have failed him, had it not been hurled in Numbers (*d*)

Longinus who writ two Treatiſes on Harmonious Compoſition, which are now loſt, makes it a Branch of the *Sublime*; and ſais, " it hath not only a na-" tural Tendency to perſwade and pleaſe, but to " inſpire us, in a wonderful Degree with a generous " Ardor and Paſſion (*e*);" attributing the ſame Effect to it as to Muſic: and illuſtrates its Efficacy by a well choſen Inſtance out of *Demoſthenes's* Oration *de Coronâ*. And how much this very Art which he recommends contributed to make his Writings an Example of that *Sublime* they deſcribe, every one of good Taſte and Judgment will eaſily ſee.

This Subject hath been handled with great Nicety and Refinement by *Demetrius Phalareus*, *Dionyſius* of *Halicarnaſſus*, and *Quintilian*; eſpecially the two laſt (the former of which lived about fifty, and the latter about an hundred and fifty Years after *Cicero*) have made many curious Obſervations upon it; ſome of which I ſhall hereafter make Uſe of. And the Engliſh Reader would be really ſurprized to ſee with what Exactneſs they lay down Rules concerning

B 2   Times,

(*d*) *Quaſi verò Trallianus fuerit Demoſthenes: cujus non tam vibrarent fulmina illa, niſi numeris contorta ferrentur.* Cic. Orat. ad finem.
(*e*) Ὀυ μόνον ἐςὶ πειθῦς καὶ ἡδονῆς ἡ Ἁρμονία φυσικὸν ἀνθρώποις ἐνέργημα, ἀλλὰ καὶ μετ' ἐλευθερίας καὶ πάθες θαυμαςόν τι ὄργανον. *Longin. de Sublim.* Sect. 38. § 39.

Times, Feet, and Measures, in Prose as well as Verse; and how nicely they examine and anatomise Sentences, Words, Syllables, and even Letters, to find out the most soft and pleasing Sounds to improve the Harmony of the Composition.

It must be acknowledged indeed that after the Dissolution of the Roman Republick, this Art began to be perverted by being too much admired. Men grew excessively fond of the numerous Stile, and readily sacrificed the Strength and Energy of their Discourse to the Harmony and Cadence of their Language. *Pliny* the younger often complains of this contemptible Affectation. And *Quintillian* speaks of certain Prose-Writers in his Time, who boasted that their Compositions were so strictly Numerous, that their Hearers might even beat Time to their Measures. And it should seem that even in *Tully*'s Time this Matter was carryed to Excess; since even then the Orators dealt so much in Numbers, that it was made a Question, wherein they differed from the Poets.

But this was a manifest Abuse of the Art; which in itself is so far from being Effeminate that it not only adds Grace but Strength to the Powers of Perswasion: otherwise it had never been so much studied, recommended and practised by all the great Orators among the Antients.

However it must be owned that if the Antients carried this Matter to an Extreme one Way, the Moderns have run into as great another. If *they* too much admired this Art, *these* to much neglect it. Harmony in Prose Compositions seems now to be little understood; and the Principles from whence it it flows still less. Many modern Writers, and those of no inconsiderable Name, are so very incurious in this Point, that provided there be Grammar and Thought they seem concerned for nothing else. As if a graceful Stile did not shew a fine Thought to as much Advantage as a decent Dress does a fine Gentleman. Intrinsick Excellence will not excuse a negligent Slovenliness in either. Hence it is (as *Dionysius* (*f*) observes) that we see the Language of one Writer low and creeping, of another mutilated and broken, of another shamefully coarse and deformed; which is owing not altogether to an ill Choice of Words (as some are apt to think) but oftentimes to a mere Neglect of Numbers; and which perhaps might be intirely rectifyed with Regard to some particular Periods, only by the Omission or Transposition of a single Word.

I would not however in what I say be thought to prefer the Beauty of Elocution to that of Sentiment; which last is as much preferable to the first, as a Jewel is to the Casket that contains it. But why may not a precious Stone be well polished and well set? And who is not sensible of its superior Lustre when it is so?

Several Writers have taken Notice of this Defect in our modern Compositions. Dr. *Pemberton* speaking of the Numbers in the Greek and Latin Tongues sais, " that these Measures were of such Efficacy in those Languages, that the adjusting their " Periods to some agreeable Rhythmus or Movement, by an apt Succession of long and short " Syllables,

---

(*f*) Οἷς δὲ μὴ ἐγένετο πρόνοια τῦ[τ]ε μέρος, οἱ μὲν ταπεινὰς, οἱ δὲ κατακεκλασμένας, οἱ δὲ ἄλλην τινὰ αἰσχύνην ἢ ἀμορφίαν ἐχούσας ἐξήνεγκαν τὰς γραφάς. *Dionys. Halicarn. de Struct. Orat. Sect.* xviii.

"Syllables, was confidered in Oratory as an Art of
" great Importance towards the Perfection of Elo-
" quence. In our Language this feems to be fcarce
" thought of; though perhaps, what we common-
" ly call Smoothnefs of Style is in Part owing to
" fomething Analagous; namely fuch a Arrange-
" ment of the Words whereby the Syllables follow
" one another with a free and eafy Cadence (*g*)."

Another Author, who for his numerous Stile is one of the firft among the Moderns, and, I think, fecond to few of the Antients, juftly obferves, " that
" among the principal Defects of our Englifh Ora-
" tors, their general Difregard of Harmony has, I
" think, been the leaft obferved. It would be In-
" juftice indeed to deny that we have fome Perform-
" ances of this Kind among us tolerably Mufical;
" but it muft be acknowledged at the fame Time,
" that it is more the Effect of Accident than De-
" fign; and rather a Proof of the Power of our
" Language than the Art of our Orarors." One probable Reafon which he affigns for this Neglect is, " that poffibly that Strength of Underftanding
" and Solidity of Reafon, which is fo eminently
" our national Characteriftick may add fomething
" to the Difficulty of reconciling us to a Study of
" this Kind; as at firft Glance it may feem to lead
" an Orator from his grand and principal Aim; and
" tempt him to make a Sacrifice of Senfe to Sound."
——In Reply to which he adds—— " that *Tully*
" and *Quintillian*, thofe great Mafters of numerous
" Compofition, have laid it down as a fixt and in-
" variable Rule, that it muft never appear the Ef-
" fect of Labour in the Orator; that it is the high-
" eft

(*g*) Obfervations on Poetry, Sect. 12.

" eſt Offence againſt the Art to weaken the Ex-
" preſſion in Order to give a more muſical Tone
" to the Cadence; that the tuneful Flow of the
" Periods muſt always ſeem caſual; in ſhort, that
" no unmeaning Words are to be thrown in merely
" to fill up the requiſite Meaſure, but that they
" muſt ſtill riſe in Senſe as they improve in Sound (*h*)."
Which Rule is here very happily exemplifyed in
the very Words that deſcribe it.

Others have imagined that our Language is not
capable of being refined and beautifyed in this Manner. " The free Language we ſpeak (ſais an inge-
nious Author) will not endure ſuch refined Regula-
" tions, for Fear of Incumbrance and Reſtraint.
" Harmony indeed it is capable of to a high Degree,
" yet ſuch as flows not from Precept, but the Ge-
" nius and *Judgment* of Compoſers. A good Ear
" is worth a thouſand Rules; ſince with it the
" Periods will be rounded and ſweetened, and the
" Stile exalted, ſo that Judges ſhall commend and
" teach others to admire; and without it, all En-
" deavours to gain Attention ſhall be Vain and In-
" effectual, unleſs where the Grandeur of the
" Senſe will atone for rough and unharmonious Ex-
" preſſion (*i*)."

But in what Senſe our Language is capable of
Harmony to a high Degree, and yet *will not endure* thoſe *Regulations* that are neceſſary to it; or
how it can flow from the *Judgment* of the Compoſers without ſome Rule to direct that *Judgment*
(for Judgment implys ſome Rule to judge by) I
do

(*h*) *Fitzoſbourn*'s Letters. Letter 24.
(*i*) *Smith*'s Notes and Obſervations on *Longinus*. p. 183.

do not very clearly conceive.——*A good Ear is worth a thousand Rules.*——'Tis true; so it is in Music. But an Acquaintance with the musical Notes and Chords, and the Rules and Principles of Harmony is notwithstanding necessary to make a good Musician. If we are to have no Rules, what must they do that have no Ear? And the best Ear may sometimes receive very proper Correction from Precept.

In short, this learned Author must mean, either that the Rules relating to numerous Composition so accurately laid down by the Antients, are not applicable to our Language; or if they are, there is no Need of them. But which ever of these he means (for he does not expressly say which, but seems to intimate both) the direct Contrary, I believe, will appear to the Reader in the Sequel of this Treatise. The Design of which is to shew, that the Rules and Principles of this Art, which was so much the Study and Admiration of the Greek and Roman Writers, are as Applicable to our Language as theirs, and in what Manner they are to be actually applyed in Order to Improve the Harmony of Prose Composition.

CHAP.

CHAP. II.

The Nature and Quality of simple Numbers or Feet, seperately considered.

THE simple Feet are these following

    Feet of two Syllables.

Pyrrhic	ᴗ ᴗ
Iambic	ᴗ —
Trochee	— ᴗ
Spondee	— —

    Feet of three Syllables.

Tribrachys	ᴗ ᴗ ᴗ
Dactyl	— ᴗ ᴗ
Amphibrachys	ᴗ — ᴗ
Anapæst	ᴗ ᴗ —
Bacchic	ᴗ — —
Cretic	— ᴗ —
Palimbacchic	— — ᴗ
Molossus	— — — (*k*)

These Numbers, considered in themselves or unconnected with any other, are either Generous and Strong, or Base and Weak.

(*k*) For a more particular Account of the several Numbers both simple and compound, See *The Essay on the Power and Principles of Harmony in Verse*, Chap. vi.

The generous Numbers are these,

Iambic	⏑ —
Spondee	— —
Anapæst	⏑ ⏑ —
Cretic	— ⏑ —
Bacchic	⏑ — —
Molossus	— — —

The base Numbers are these (*l*).

Pyrrhic	⏑ ⏑
Trochee	— ⏑
Tribrachys	⏑ ⏑ ⏑
Dactyl	— ⏑ ⏑ (*m*)
Amphibrachys	⏑ — ⏑
Palimbacchic	— — ⏑

These

(*l*) When we call these Feet base, low and feeble, we only mean when they are taken by themselves; for when they are judiciously blended with others, they are of equal Importance with the rest, and (like Mortar in a Building) contribute as much to the Strength and Beauty of the Composition. Which *Quintillian* does not seem to have attended to, when he blamed *Dionysius* and other Writers before him for making this Distinction. [*Miror autem* (fais he) *in hac Opinione doctissimos homines fuisse, ut alios pedes ita eligerent, alios damnarent, quasi ullus esset quem non sit necesse in oratione deprehendi.* De Instit. Orat. l. ix, c. 4.] For certain it is that these Feet which are called Base, Weak, and Low, are really so, when taken by themselves or only with themselves, and not intermixt with those of better Quality.

(*m*) Though *Dionysius* calls this σεμνὸς, *i. e.* a grave and venerable Foot, yet he only means when it is taken in Conjunction with the Spondee, which corrects and tempers it. And thus he immediately explains himself, καὶ εἰς κάλλος ἁρμονίας ἀξιολογώτατος, καὶ τό γε ἡρωϊκὸν μέτρον ἀπὸ τῦ κοσμεῖται ὡς ἐπὶ τὸ πολύ. De Struct. Orat. Sect. xvii. *i. e.* it's very well fitted to Harmonize the Verse, and to be an Ornament to the Heroic Measure; where it is always mixt with Spondees. But of itself it is too light and feeble, and never fit to End a Verse. And therefore those Measures that admit it, always require for a Close one

These Numbers are called generous or base, because the Movement of the one is Sublime and Strong, and that of the other Low and Feeble.

Now this different Movement of the Feet depends upon two Things.

(1.) The different Quantities or Number of Time they contain, for a Foot that consists of more Times is ordinarily more Magnificent than one that consists of fewer. *e. g.* A Spondee (--) is more noble than a Pyrrhic (⌣⌣), because that consists of four Times, and this but of two; and a Molossus (---) more noble than a Tribrachys (⌣⌣⌣) because the former hath double the Times of the latter.

(2.) Another Thing on which the different Movement of the Feet depends, is the Quantity of the Syllable with which it ends; for a Foot that ends with a long Syllable is more Strong and Sonorous, and consequently more Noble and Generous, than one that terminates in a short one. Thus an Iambic (⌣-), is more noble than a Trochee (-⌣); an Anapæst (⌣⌣-), than a Dactyl (-⌣⌣): Though the Trochee contains just the same Number of Times as the Iambic, and the Anapæst as the Dactyl. So that in this Case the Excellence of one above the other depends altogether on the Quantity of the final Syllable.

But here let it be remarked, that of those which I call the generous or the noble Feet, some are more excellent than others; which is occasioned by a short Syllable preceeding the final long one. And this

---

one or two long Syllables to qualify it; as in the Latin *Hexameters,* and the English Dactylic Measure. See *the Essay on the Power &c, of Harmony in Verse,* Chap xix.

this indeed makes a more confiderable Difference in the Nature of the Feet, than the Difference of Times they contain. Hence an Iambic (◡–) is reckoned a better Foot than a Spondee (– –), though the latter contains the moſt Times; and for the fame Reafon the Anapæſt (◡◡–) is more excellent than the Moloſſus (– – –); becaufe the final long Syllable is rendered more diſtinct ſtrong and emphatical by coming immediately after a ſhort one.

Hence then it follows that the Iambic (◡–) is the moſt noble and generous of all the Feet (*n*); and that the reſt have their Degree of Excellence in Proportion as they approach to or recede from it, in the following Order, Iambic (◡–), Anapæſt (◡◡–), Cretic (–◡–), Bacchic (◡– –), Spondee (– –), Moloſſus (– – –).

And it is obfervable that this Order or Difpofition, *viz.* that a quick ſhould be fucceeded by a flow Movement, is univerfally agreeable. For as a long Time is beſt after a ſhort one, fo is a long Foot after a ſhort one, a long Word after the ſhort ones (*o*), even as the flow Meafures in Verfe, and the flow Airs in Mufic come in moſt agreeably after the quick ones. This is as pleafing to the Ear as Reſt

after

(*n*) Hence *Ariſtotle* fais that in his Time it was more ufed than any other Number by thofe who fpake in Public. Αὕτη ἐςιν ἡ λέξις ἡ τῶν πολλῶν. Διὸ μάλιςα πάντων τῶν μέτρων ἰαμβεῖα φθέγγονται λέγοντες. Rhetor l. 3. c. 8. And again in his *Poetics*, Ex omnibus Metris Sermoni quotidiano accommodatum maximè eſt *Iambicum.* Cui rei id ſigno eſt, quod plurima nos Iambica proferamus imprudentes in Collocutione mutuâ. *Ariſt. Poet. c.* 2. *None of all the Meafures run more naturally into our common Speech than the Iambic; as appears from hence, that in our ordinary Converfation we often fpeak in* IAMBICS, *before we are fenfible of it.*

(*o*) *Ideoque etiam brevium Verborum ac Nominum vitanda Continuatio, et ex diverfo quoque longorum: afferunt enim quandam dicendi Tarditatem.* Quint. l. ix. c. 4.

after Motion is to Nature. If it be enquired, whence the Agreeableness of this Order arises, or on what Principles in Nature it is founded; this Mystery perhaps lies too deep for our Discovery: Let it suffice that universal Experience verifies the Observation.

Another Thing that deserves to be observed on this Subject is, that as some of the generous Feet are more noble than others, so they have each of them their respective Qualities. *e. g.* A Spondee (- -) is a grave and majestick Foot (*p*); *Molossus* (- - -) sublime and stately (*q*); *Bacchic* (⌣ - -) strong and solemn (*r*); a *Cretic* (- ⌣ -) is a bold and eager Foot (*s*); the *Anapæst* (⌣ ⌣ -) rapid and vehement; excellently adapted to martial Music and martial Songs, which are therefore frequently set to this Measure. *e. g.*

With Hearts bold and stout

We'll repel the vile rout,

And follow fair Liberty's Call;

We'll

(*p*) *Hebetior videtur et tardior, habet tamen stabilem quendam et non expertem Dignitatis gradum.* Cic. Orat. Ed. Lond. Tom. 1. p 166.

(*q*) Ὑψηλός δὲ καὶ ἀξιωματικός ἐστι, καὶ διαβεβηκὼς ὡς ἐπὶ πολύ. Dion. Hal. de Struct. Orat. Sect. xvii.

(*r*) So called, because in this Kind of Measure the *Dithyrambic* Poets used to rant out their Songs in Honour of *Bacchus*. What is here called *Bacchic*, *Dionysius* calls Hypobacchic; and terms it, ὁ ῥυθμὸς ἀξίωμα ἔχων καὶ μέγεθος. Ibid.

(*s*) Because it approaches near to the Iambic, and (as *Tully* observes) sounds to the Ear pretty much like the *fourth Pæon*, or *Pæon posterior*. (⌣ ⌣ ⌣ -) as it contains the same Number of Times; and all the Difference between them is, that the two short Syllables in the Beginning of the Latter are contracted into one long one in the Beginning of the Former. *De Oratore*, l. 3.

We'll rush on the Foe,

And deal Death in each Blow,

Till Conquest and Honour crown all.

And *Tully* tells us it is the Measure in which the Roman Generals were wont to harangue their Men (*t*); as nothing is better fitted to excite the Passions (*u*). And the *Iambic* (which is of all the Numbers most generous) is very strong and sonorous, very proper (as *Horace* observes) to excite and express the Passion of Anger (*v*). Hence the *Anapæst* and *Iambic* are not improperly called by some, the *pushing Numbers*.

And how naturally the Spondee, Anapæst and Iambic (which are the most bold, strong and sonorous Feet) do run into a Martial Air, may be seen in the Margin, which demonstrates the Qualities that have been just assigned them (*w*).

The

(*t*) *Nec adhebitur ulla sine Anapæstis Pedibus Hortatio.* Tuscul. Quæst. l. ii. c. 16.

(*u*) Ἀνάπαιστος σεμνότητα δὲ ἔχει πολλήν, καὶ ἔνθα δεῖ μέγεθος περιθέναι τοῖς πράγμασιν ἢ πάθος ἐπιτήδειός ἐστι παραλαμβάνεσθαι. Dion. Hal. de Struct. Orat. Sect. xvii.

(*v*) *Archilocum proprio rabies armavit Iambo.* Art. Poet. l. 79. So *Quintilian*, Aspero contrà Iambis maximè concitantur: non solum quòd sint a duobus modò Syllabis, eoque frequentiorem quasi Pulsum habent, quæ res lenitati contraria est; sed etiam quod omnibus partibus insurgunt, et a brevibus in longas nituntur et crescunt. *De Inst. Orat.* l. ix. c. 4. Arist. Poet. c. 2.

(*w*) The double double Beat

Of the thundering Drum

Crys

[15]

The Drum is an Inftrument which in a wonderful Manner fhews the Force and Power of Poetic Numbers; for though its Sound be only a Monotony, yet it exactly expreffes all the different Qualities of the feveral Feet. And when we beat thofe Numbers upon it, only by varying the Movement into quicker or flower, and making the Sound ftronger or fofter, the Mind is affected as much as it is by an Inftrument that runs all the Notes of the *Gamut*.

Let us try then if we cannot, by imitating the Sound of this Inftrument, exemplify the different Qualities of the feveral Feet as before defcribed; by giving both to the bafe and the generous Numbers all the Advantage they can receive from Order or the Succeffion of the long Syllables after the fhort ones.

The bafe Numbers are thefe, Pyr: Troch: Tribr: Dact: Amphibr: Palimbac:

And

Crys, *Heark!* the Foe's come:
Charge! Charge! 'tis too late to retreat!
Say's Effay the fecond, p. 167.

This will be more manifeft by beating thefe feveral Numbers in proper time upon a Drum, *e. g.*

Titum tititum tumtum tumtum tititum,

Tititum tumtum titum tumtum;

Titum tumtum tititum tumtum tititum.

Now every Word, except a Monofyllable, is compofed of fome Foot or Feet (*x*); the right Difpofition of which is that which conftitutes what is *properly* called a *numerous Stile*. For though any Combination of Words may be reduced into their refpective Numbers of which they are compofed, yet unlefs thofe Numbers be well adjufted or agreeably intermixed; it is not called a *numerous*, but a *rough, lame* or *broken* Stile (*y*).

But a fmooth and flowing is not the only numerous Stile; that which is rough, mafculine and vehement hath fometimes an equal Claim to that Title; provided the Sound of the Numbers conform to the Senfe of the Words. To deny this, is in Effect to affirm that there is no Mufick but what is foft, and no Verfe but what is fmooth. If the Senfe be fublime and ftrong, the Numbers fhould be flow and ftately. And be the Senfe what it will, the Words fhould in fome Degree be an *Eccho* to it, in Profe as well as Verfe. On this Score it is that Horace,

---

(*x*) Πᾶν ὄνομα καὶ ῥῆμα καὶ ἄλλο μόριον λέξεως, ὅ,τι μὴ μονοσυλλαβόν ἐστιν, ἐν ῥυθμῷ τινὶ λέγεται. —*Dion. Hal.* de Struct. Orat. Sect. xvii.

(*y*) *Sed omnis nec claudicans, nec quafi fluctuans, et æqualiter confluenterque ingrediens, numerofa habetur Oratio.* Cic. Orat. That Stile (fais *Tully*) which hath not a limping irregular Movement but a uniform conftant Flow, is called a numerous Stile.——But his Meaning in what prefently follows, I confefs I do not apprehend; where he fais, *Idque quod numerofum in Oratione dicitur non femper numero fiat fed nonnunquam aut concinnitate aut conftructione Verborum.* Id. Ed. Lond. T. 1. p. 167. a. *i.e.* That a numerous Stile is not always owing to the Numbers, but fometimes to a certain neat Conftruction of the Words.—— But what that agreeable Conftruction of the Words can be owing to, but the Numbers of which they are Compofed, I am at a Lofs to guefs.—— Unlefs he means (as perhaps he may) that there are fome Words of fo harfh and jarring a Sound, that when they meet (though they may compofe a good Number yet) cannot be pronounced without fome Difficulty: Which indeed is fometimes the Cafe.

Horace, notwithstanding the Roughness and Irregularity of some of his Measures, especially in his *Satires*, may be deemed, what the smoother *Ovid* calls him, a *numerous* Writer (*z*).

Were we (as *Dionysius* (*a*) observes) to use none but the best and most generous Numbers, our Stile would be always Musical; that is, either soft and flowing, or grave and majestick. But as we are obliged for the Sake of Aptitude of Expression to make Use of Words that introduce the weak and feeble Numbers, which tend to break the Harmony and debase the Majesty of our Language, the great Art lies in mixing and disposing of those baser Numbers in such a Manner as that the Harshness of them shall give no Offence to a good Ear; which in this Case is a very sovereign and critical Judge. And this is done chiefly by mixing them with as much good Company as we can; I mean with better Numbers: And disposing of them into those Places where they will be least attended to, that is in the Middle of a Period, and keeping them by all Means from the End of it, where the Ear always expects to be pleased.

Every Sentence may be conceived as divisible into distinct and seperate Clauses; every Clause where there is an apparent Cessation of the Voice, should always End with a generous Foot; and all the preceding Numbers be so intermixt, that the short ones be duly qualified by the succeeding long ones; reserving the best and most harmonious Numbers for the Cadence. And this, in short, is what constitutes

---

(*z*) *Sæpe tenet nostras numerosus Horatius Aures.*
See *Say's* Essay, p. 116.
(*a*) De Struct. Orat. Sect. xviii.

tutes that agreeable Fluency of Words which in Profe we call a fmooth and pleafant Stile; and which, if at the fame Time it be clear and expreffive, hath all the Elegance of which Profe-Compofition is capable. To illuftrate this by one plain Inftance. A late Divine fpeaking of the Trinity hath this Expreffion — *It is a Myftery which we firm|ly be|lieve the | Truth of, | and hum|bly a|dore the | Depth of.*—Here the Language is expreffive but not harmonious. And what is the Reafon of this? Not merely becaufe each Claufe of the Sentence ends with the Sign of the Genitive Cafe (which, if it be fometimes deemed an Inaccuracy, yet does not always interrupt the fmooth Flow of the Words) but becaufe it is compofed almoft intirely of bafe and feeble Numbers, *viz. Pyrrhics* and *Trochees*; as appears from the Reduction of them; which by a fmall Tranfpofition of the Words might eafily be avoided. As thus —— *It is a Myftery, the Truth | of which | we firm|ly believe |, and the Depth | of which | we hum|bly adore.|* Every Ear will foon determine this to be the moft agreeable Diction. And the Reafon why it is fo is now very plain. Becaufe according to this Difpofition of the Words, the Sentence is compofed altogether of ftrong and generous Feet, *viz. Iambics* and *Anapæfts*. But the Method of reducing the Members of a Profe Period into the original Numbers of which they are compofed, will be more particularly confidered in the following Chapter.

But before I conclude this, it may not be amifs to obferve, that this is the only Reafon, that in all

all Languages (especially the learned ones) we find the Words so frequently transposed out of their natural Order; *viz.* to give them a softer Flow, a stronger Sound, or smoother Cadence, by reserving the most sweet, strong and generous Numbers for the Close. For which end such a Transposition is always allowable, provided it do not by being too frequent, stiffen the Stile, obscure the Sense, or seem affected.

CHAP. III.

Concerning the Manner of reducing Prosaic Numbers, or examining the Feet of which any Period is composed.

HERE we are to take *Dionysius* for our Guide; who hath shewn us in various Instances how Prosaic Numbers are to be reduced (c). To take one out of many, let us see in what Manner he examines the Numbers of that celebrated Speech of *Thucydides*, which he affirms to be so full of Grandeur and Dignity, and begins thus — Οἱ μὲν | πολλοὶ | τῶν ἐρ|θάδε ἤ|δη εἰ|ρηκό]ων, | ἐπαινοῦ|σι τὸν προσ|θέντα τῷ | νόμῳ τὸν | λόγον τόν|δε. — Now that which gives such an Air of Majesty to this Sentence (sais he) is, that each Member of it is composed of the most sublime and generous Feet. For in the first Member, which ends with the Word εἰρηκότων, the three first Feet are *Spondees*, the fourth an *Anapæst*, the fifth a *Spondee*, and the sixth

(c) De Struct. Orat. Sect. xviii.

sixth a *Cretic*. And in the second Member of the Sentence, which begins with the Word ἐταινίαις, the two first Feet are *Bacchics* (which he calls *Hypobacchics*) the third a *Cretic*, and the two last Feet *Bacchics*; the whole concluding with an odd Syllable, which is common.

Now here I would make the following Observations.

(1.) That in reducing Prose-Sentences into their Original Numbers, there is no Necessity to confine ourselves to Dissyllable Feet only.

For in reducing the first Member of this Sentence, *Dionysius* uses both the Dissyllable and Trissyllable Feet: But it is capable of being reduced into all dissyllable Numbers; thus— Ο͝ι μεν | πολλοι | των ενθαδε | ηδ'η | ειρη|χοτων. And according to this Method of Reduction you see there is but one feeble Foot among them, *viz.* the *Pyrrhic* in the fourth Place; and even this is not at all amiss, as it is there situated; for the *Spondee* immediately following corrects its Rapidity, and gives it the agreeable Air of an *Anapæst*.

Therefore (11.) In examining the Numbers of a Prosaic Period, it is usually the best Way to reduce them into Feet of three Syllables rather than those of two.

For this Reason; because though there may be several weak and base dissyllable Feet in it, yet as they stand in Conjunction with others of a better Quality, they are strengthened and harmonised, and become very good Feet of three or four Syllables.
Thus

[23]

Thus the *Pyrrhic* and the *Trochee*, though they are both weak and feeble Numbers of themselves, yet followed by a *Spondee* they gather Force, and the one has the Air of an *Anapæst* and the other of a *Cretic*, which are both good triſſyllable Feet. And therefore *Dionyſius*, you obſerve, reſolves the ſecond Member of the Sentence into all *Triſſyllables*; by which Diviſion they appear to be all ſtrong and generous Numbers. Whereas were they to be divided all into Diſſyllables thus— επαι|νωσι|τον προσθει]α τω νομω τον| λογον| τονδε,—there would appear to be no leſs than three *Trochees*, which of themſelves are baſe and feeble Feet; and might tempt us to think that the Numbers were not good. But being all ſucceeding by a long Syllable, they are exalted and confirmed, and aſſume the Grace and Force of a *Cretic*, which is a good triſſyllable Foot.

(III.) The laſt Syllable of a Proſe Sentence, like that of a Verſe, is always common; that is, may be conſidered as long or ſhort, as it beſt ſuits the Cloſe.

For this we have *Tully*'s Authority (*d*). *Quintilian* indeed pretends that his Ear could diſtinguiſh whether the laſt Syllable of a Sentence be long or

---

(*d*) Nihil enim ad rem, extrema illa, longa ſit, an brevis *Orat.*: and therefore he makes the Word *perſolutas* as well as *comprobavit* to be a *Dichoree*, which he recommends as no bad cloſe. But when he commends a double *Trochee* for a good cloſe, it's much he ſhou'd condemn a ſingle *Trochee* for a bad one; eſpecially ſince it may be conſidered as a Spondee, by his allowing the laſt Syllable to be common. And yet we find he does, in theſe Words, *ſed eò* (Trochéus) *vitioſus in òràtióne ſi ponatur Extremus, quod Verba melius in Syllabas longiores cadunt.* Id. p. 166. (*b*).

or short (*e*). And perhaps it might; but I see no Necessity to descend to such extreme Refinements. Therefore

(IV.) The last Syllable being common, it is often neglected and made no Account of (especially if it be naturally short) and serves only to give a Grace or Flourish to the preceeding long one, and may be considered in the same Quality as a double Rhime in the End of a Verse. Thus in the last Word of the Sentence before us (τόνδε), the Syllable (δε) you see is detached from the final Foot, or rather considered as belonging to the last Syllable, as a Part of it.

This odd Syllable at the Close which cannot conveniently be taken into the last Number is called by the Greeks κατάληξις; of which *Dionysius* gives us several Instances in | the Place | above | refer'd | to. But

(V.) What is chiefly to be remarked in the Method in which *Dionysius* reduces the above Sentence is this, (*viz.*) hence it appears that the Greeks read their Prose as well as their Verse by the *Quantity* and not by the *Accent*; that is, in Pronunciation they laid the Stress or Force of their Voice on the long Syllables though they were not accented, and slurred quickly over the short ones though they were.

For *Dionysius* here reduces the Numbers according as they were pronounced. And in the first Clause

---

(*e*) Quamvis habeatur indifferens ultima——aures tamen consulens meas intelligo multum referre, utrumne longa fit quæ cludit, an pro longâ. De Inst. Orat. l. ix. c. 4. p. 486.

[25]

Clause in the Words ἐνθάδε and εἰρηκότων, though the Syllable (θά) in the former, and (κό) in the latter are both accented, yet according to the Disposition of the Numbers here given us, we find they are both pronounced short, and read thus ἐνθάδε εἰρηκότων. So in the last Member we find the first Syllable of the Word νόμῳ and that of the Word λόγον were both pronounced short, though both accented, and read thus νόμῳ, λόγον. This therefore (after all that hath been said upon the Subject) to me appears a Demonstration, that with Regard to the Stress or Emphasis of the Pronunciation, the Antients read by the *Quantity only.*   ✗

If it be said, of what Use then were the Accents? I answer, they were designed very probably at first to regulate the Tone or Key of the Voice, not the Stress or Force of it, which are two very different Things; or to shew when the Voice is to be elevated or depressed; that is, not when it is to be stronger or weaker, but higher or lower, acute or grave, according as the Accent directed. This, as it is extremely difficult for us to imitate them herein, and would answer no good Purpose that I know of if we could, is sufficient to justify us in paying them no Regard at all, and furnishes us with a good Reason to read Greek Prose as well as Poetry, according to the *Quantity only* as the Greeks themselves did.

Let us take another Instance out of the same Author (p. 139.) and see how he reduces the following Sentence of *Plato*.—ἂν τυχόντες πορεύονται | τὴν εἱμαρμένην | πορείαν. Here (sais he) the two first Feet are *Critics,*

E   then

then follow two *Spondees*, then a *Cretic*, and lastly a *Bacchic*. So that here again he uses both dissyllable and trisyllable Feet. And his calling the three last Syllables of the Word εἱμαρμένη a *Cretic*, it is plain he read it thus ειμαρμενην, without any Regard to the Accent on the Penultima (μέ).

After this Example now let us examine the Feet in the English Translation of the two first Verses of the Bible, and we shall presently see how much the Grandeur of the Stile is owing to the Strength and Magnificence of the Numbers, in which the Translators are often very happy.

In the Be|ginning | God creat|ed the Heavens | and the Earth, | and the Earth | was without | Form and void; | and Darkness | was upon | the Face | of the Deep.

These three Sentences thus reduced, appear to be made up of all the most generous Feet, *viz.* the Spondee, Cretic, Molossus, Bacchic, Iambic and Anapæst, without one weak or faultering Foot among them; unless it be the first, which is a Dactyl. And that being corrected by a long Syllable immediately succeeding, becomes a good initial Number.

CHAP.

CHAP. V.

Concerning the most proper Feet to close a Sentence.

THE Antients (who I think have refined this Science to Excess) have laid down several Rules concerning the most proper Initial Numbers. Which I shall not trouble the Reader with for this Reason; Because the Ear is less apprehensive of and more reconciled to a bad Rhythmus in the Beginning than it is in the End of a Sentence. And therefore as an Orator will reserve his best Thoughts, so his best Numbers to the last; that he may close with *Eclat*; in which there is much Pleasure, Propriety and Elegance.

It was a Question among the Antient Orators, Whether the whole Period should be composed in Numbers, or only the Beginning and End of it? That is, whether an Orator is obliged to study and attend to the just Disposition of his Numbers throughout the whole Sentence, or only in the two Extremes of it. *Tully* is for the former Part of the Question, but thinks that Care should be taken to reserve the best Numbers 'till last: And gives this Reason for it; Because (fais he) the Ear, which is always waiting for the Close of the Sentence, wants to be gratified then, and therefore should not be disappointed of the Pleasure it expects (*f*). And besides

---

(*f*) Cum Aures Extremum semper expectent, in eoque acquiescant, id vacare numero (i. e. generoso) non oportet. Orat. Ed. Lond. T. 1. p. 166. b.

sides (as *Quintilian* (g) well observes) the Ear is more at leisure and more disposed to Judge of the concluding, than it is of the intermediate Numbers.

Now the several Closes recommended by the Antients are these.

(I.) A *Dichoree*, or double Trochee. This Close was approved by *Tully* and *Quintilian* (h), and was much in Use among the Greeks. And it was chiefly on Account of this sweet and decent Close (as *Tully* observes) that the following Sentence was received with such incredible Applause.—*Patris Dictum sapiens, Temeritas filii* comprobavit (i).

But it ought to be observed that as the last Syllable is common, it may be considered as long, and then the three last Syllables will be a *Bacchic*: Again, as the last Syllable may be considered as καταληξις or supernumerary, then the three preceeding Syllables will be a *Cretic*; both which are strong and generous Feet. And this is the Reason that a *Dichoree* though it be in itself a base and feeble Foot yet makes a Close so graceful.

The same may be said

(II.) Of a *Dactyl*. Because the last Syllable being common, the concluding Foot may be considered

---

(g) Quòd Aures continuam Vocem secutæ ductæque velut prono decurrentis Orationes Flumine, tum magis judicant cum ille Impetus stetit et intuendi Tempus dedit. Lib. ix. c. 4.

(h) Dichoreus est ille non vitiosus in Clausulis; cadit autem per se ille ipse præclare. Id p. 167. b. Cludet et Choreus si Pes idem sibi ipsi jungetur *Quint*. l. ix. c. 4.

(i) *Orat*. Id.

ed either as a *Dactyl* or a *Cretic* (k), and is very well preceeded by a Cretic or an Iambic; as is obferv'd by *Quintilian* (l).

Mr. *Manwaring* afferts that a Cretic before a Dactyl makes a good Clofe, *e. g. What will this End in but treacherous Knavery*: But that a Spondee before a Dactyl is bad, and gives this Inftance, *What will this End in but downright Knavery?* But on what Rule, Authority or Reafon he builds his laft Affertion, I know not. If the Ear be Judge, the latter Clofe is altogether as good as the former (*).

(III.) An *Iambic*, As this is the moft noble and generous of all the Feet, there is no one that makes a finer Clofe, efpecially if (as *Quintilian* (m) obferves) it be preceeded by a *Bacchic*; which forms a Foot of five Syllables called *Dochymus* (⌣–––⌣) and is the fame as an *Iambic* and *Cretic*. This is a firm ftately clofe. And a Spondee preceeding a final Iambic always ftands very well.

And as an Iambic is fo fine a Clofe, all thofe compound Feet that end with an Iambic, muft of Confequence be fo too. *e. g.*

(1.) A Ca-

(k) Nihil enim intereft, Dactylus fit extremus, an Creticus: quia poftrema Syllaba, brevis an longa fit, ne in verfu quidem refert. *Id.*
(l) L. ix. c. 4.
(*) See his *Harmony*, &c. p. 26.
(m) Quint. l ix. c. 4.

(1.) A Cretic. Which *Tully* allows to be a good final Foot.

(2.) Some have recommended the *Pæon Posterior* (⌣⌣⌣-) which contains the same Number of Times as the Cretic, but one Syllable more, and is composed of a Pyrrhic and Iambic, as a Foot that Closes admirably well (*n*). But *Tully* prefers a Cretic before it for a Close; which, if the Ear may be a Judge, is a much better Foot (*o*).

(3.) An Anapest is a good final Foot, as it ends in an Iambic. And as it's two first Syllables are short, it is best preceeded by one that is long.

(iv.) A Spondee makes a good Close. It may be preceeded

(1.) By a short Syllable; and then it becomes a Bacchic. Or

(2.) By a long one; and then it becomes a Molossus; a very majestic Foot.

(3.) By

(*n*) *Say's* Essay. p. 108.

(*o*) And the other, which is called the *first Pæon* (-⌣⌣⌣) consisting of a Trochee and a Pyrrhic, and is nothing else than the former Pæon reversed, is recommended by some as a good initial Foot; See *Say's* Essay. p. 108. *Quint.* p. 487. And these Movements *Aristotle* thinks are peculiar to Prose; because no Verse can be formed of them. For being in the Sesquialterate Proportion (*i. e.* as 2 to 3) they are not capable of being regularly measured by the Hand *per Arsin et Thesin*. Vid *Aristot. Rhetoric.* l. 3. c. 8. *Essay on Numbers*, &c. Chap. vii.

(3.) By a Trochee; and then it becomes the firſt Epitrite (‒ ◡ ‒ ‒) a Cloſe which *Tully* much delights in (*p*).

(4.) By a Cretic. *Quintilian* well approves this Cloſe (*q*).

(5.) By an Anapæſt. This is but barely admitted by the Author before mentioned, (*r*).

(6.) By a Dactyl. This indeed is condemn'd by *Quintilian* for this Reaſon; becauſe (ſais he) " a Proſe " Period ſhould never conclude like the Line of a " Verſe, (*s*)." But as this refer'd to the Latin Hexameters, and is not the proper Cloſe of Engliſh Verſe, we

---

(*p*) See his Oration *pro lege Manilâ.*——Urbemque &c. L. Luculli Virtute Aſſiduitate, Conſilio, ſummis Obſidionis Periculis, *liberatam* : patefactumque noſtris Legionibus *eſſe pontum*; qui antè populo Romano ex omni aditu *clauſus eſſet*: cæteraſque Urbes Ponti et Cappadociæ permultas, uno aditu atque adventu *eſſe captas:* Regem—ad alios ſe reges atque alias gentes ſupplicem *contuliſſe:* atque hæc omnia, ſalvis populi Romani ſociis atque integris Vectigalibus, *eſſe geſtas.* Satis opinor hoc *eſſe laudis.* Tom. i. p. 311. a.

(*q*) L. ix. c. 4. p. 487.

(*r*) Poteſt, etiamſi minus bene, præponi Anapæſtus. *Ibid.*

(*s*) Ne Dactylus quidem Spondæo bene præponitur, quia finem verſus damnamus in fine Orationis. *Id.* p. 488. The juſtneſs of this Obſervation of *Quintilian* will be conſidered hereafter.

we have not the same Reason for condemning it, And with us a Spondee preceeded by a Dactyl, stands very well at the End of a Sentence.

(7.) The same may be said of a Pyrrhic before a Spondee. The rapid Movement of the former being agreeably corrected by the Slowness of the latter.

But three short Syllables together should not be often used though succeeded by a Spondee.

And four or five together is much worse: for few Ears are reconcileable to the Rapidity of a double Pyrrhic.

(Lastly.) A Spondee in a Close may sometimes be very well succeeded by itself, which makes an extreme slow Movement. And sometimes we may use three or four Spondees successively, when we mean to fix an Impression by dwelling upon the Words that convey it.

A notable Instance of which we have in *Tully*'s Oration against *Verres*. In reciting the ignominious Punishment of a Roman Citizen, whom *Verres* had ordered to be scourged with Rods, he makes Use of this Art to raise a Horrour of the Fact in the Minds of his Hearers. The Action was so vile in itself, that the bare Recital of it was sufficient to inflame their Indignation. Which he more effectually does by by the Slowness with which thefe plain, and to all Appearance, artlefs Expreffions are pronounced, *Cædebatur virgis Civis Romanus; cum nulla Vox alia iſtius miſeri, inter dolorum crepitumque plagarum, audiebatur, niſi hæc,* Civis Romanus sum (*t*).

CHAP. VI.

Of Poetic Proſe.

A Proſe Writer may be ſaid to have a Poetic Stile,

[1.] When he makes Uſe of thoſe Images, Figures or Words, which are too bold and ſtrong to be allowed in any but Poetical Compoſitions; with a View to affect the Paſſions, rather than inform the Judgment; and in all his Paintings, ſeems more attentive to the Goodneſs of his Colours than the Juſtneſs of the Features. This turgid Stile in Poetry is called *Bombaſt:* In Proſe it is ſomething worſe.

[2.] When he binds his Periods with too much Uniformity and Strictneſs, and does not ſufficiently

---

(*t*) In Verrem, l. v. p. 295. Mr. *Manwaring* indeed affirms that there can ſcarce be a Union of two Spondees; for the Concluſion is heavy and flat. The Reaſon he gives for it indeed is ſo; and too weak by far, to ſtand in Oppoſition to the Authority juſt mentioned.
Manwaring on Harmony, p. 26, 27.

ly diversify his Numbers to throw them out of Poetical Measure. And hence it is that those who have dealt much in Verse, are so apt in their Prose Compositions to run into a Poetic Stile.

The Laws of Poetic and Prosaic Numbers are essentially different. For in Poetry we are tyed down to those Numbers only which are appropriate to that Species of Verse we write in, whether Trochaic, Anapæstic or Iambic, with only those Variations, Licences or Anomalies that are allowed by Custom, and the Authority of the best Writers in that Way. But in Prose we are tyed to no particular Sort of Numbers, but are permitted to make Use of any that are harmonious to the Ear, and form a graceful Cadence. And this is done by a judicious Intermixture of the short and long ones; or by introducing more of the one Sort or the other, according as the Subject requires.

This then being the essential Difference and just Boundary between the Prose and Poetic Stile, we may hence draw the following Corollaries.

(1.) That it is as great a Fault in Prose Stile to be too much bound, as it is in the Poetic to be too free. Therefore

(2.) That Foot from which any Species of Poetry takes its Name, ought not to be too often repeated without the Intervention of some other; because if it succeed itself immediately above three or four times, it becomes Verse, and that Kind of Verse which takes its Name from that Foot, whether Iambic or Anapæstic, &c. e. g. A late excellent and judicious Writer, whose Stile for the most Part

is

is very chaste and sweetly numerous, describing the Devotion and Piety of the Son of God, hath these Expressions; " His Time was divided between De-
" votion and Charity, conversing with God, and
" doing good to Men. The Stars by Night as
" they moved their Rounds, beheld him breathing
" out his Soul to God. The Angels, that wait-
" ed near him with delightful Wonder, observed
" a Soul burning with a Flame of Love surpas-
" sing theirs (*u*)." Here it is plain that the Iambic Numbers succeed one another so close, that they give these Periods the direct Air of Iambic Verse.

(3.) The same Foot may be often used in the same Sentence provided any other Foot intervene, so as to throw it out of Poetical Measure. Thus, a very small Alteration will throw the foregoing Sentences out of their Poetic Movement without the least Damage either to their Sound or Sense. *e. g.*
" The Stars as they moved their nightly Rounds
" beheld him breathing out his devout Soul to God;
" The Angels that waited near him, with Won-
" der and Delight, observed a Soul burning with
" a Flame of Love that surpass'd their own."

(4.) As

(*u*) See *Grove's* Works, Vol. viii. p. 184.

(4.) As the Laws of Prose Composition will not admit of above three or four of those Feet together which constitute any Species of Verse, much less will they admit of an *intire Verse* in the midst of a Prose Sentence.

Because this quite confounds the two different Compositions, breaks down the Boundary that was designed to part them, violates the Laws of Prosaic Structure, appears too much bound, and discovers an Affectation or at least an Art in the Writer, which in Prose-Composition ought by all Means to be concealed. "For (as *Quintilian* (x) observes) though Prose Composition is bound by Numbers, yet it should appear to be perfectly free. And therefore to conceal the Poetical Measure, those Feet which close a Poetical Verse (sais he) should never close a Prose Period; nor should those that begin the former begin the latter. Because the Ear will then distinguish it, and the Stile becomes too stiff and affected. But a Prose Period may begin with the same Measure with which a Verse ends, and may end with those Feet with which a Verse begins.—To bring in those Numbers into Prose which form Part of a Verse, is not right; but to bring in an intire and compleat Verse is altogether wrong (y)."

Never to begin a Prose Period with those Numbers that begin a Verse, nor conclude it with those that close

---

(x) Quamvis enim vincta sit, tamen soluta videri debet Oratio. l. ix, c. 4. p. 484.

(y) Versum in Oratione fieri, multo fœdissimum est, totum: sicut etiam in parte, deforme: utique si pars posterior in clausula deprehendatur, aut rursus prior in Ingressu. Nam quod est contra, sæpe etiam decet; quia et cludit interim optime prima pars versus, ... et ultima versuum Initio conveniunt Orationis. Id. p. 483.

close a Verse, perhaps may be deemed too severe a Law. But his condemning a compleat Verse in the Midst of Prose (that is, when it is passed upon the Reader for Prose) surely must be just. Of the same Sentiment is *Tully* (z).

Now with this Authority I am obliged to encounter that of the learned Mr. *Blackwall*, who is of another Opinion; and produces several Instances both from Greek and Latin Authors (some of which I have thrown into the (a) Margin) wherein their Prose Stile appears to run into compleat Verse; with a View to vindicate the Stile of the sacred Writers, where we sometimes find the same Thing (b).

But why so much Solicitude to vindicate the Elegance of the Apostles Language? And to ascribe to them an Art which they avowedly neglected, and expresly declared they were above making Use of in their Writings; which were to recommend themselves, not by the Eloquence of their Stile, but the Divinity of their Doctrines? However these Instances are far from proving the Point in Hand, *viz.* that it

is

(z) —— Quòd Versus in Oratione si efficitur conjunctione Verborum, Vitium est. *De Oratore* l. 3.

Versus sæpe in Oratione per Imprudentiam dicimus: quod vehementer est vitiosum.——Perspicuum est igitur, numeris adstrictam Orationem esse debere, carere Versibus. *Orator* §. 56.

(a) Ψελλέα κ̀ϳ σρεπ7οὶ κ̀ϳ ἵπποι χρυσοχάλινοι.

Xenoph.

Κηρύττειν ὅτι κ̀ϳ γείτονα χρηςὸν ἔχειν.

Plutarch.

——Urbem Romam in principio reges habuere.

Tacitus.

(b) Πᾶσα δόσις ἀγαθὴ κ̀ϳ πᾶν δώρημα τέλειον.

Jam. i. 17.

Καὶ ἣ ἡ φωνὴ γῆν ἐσάλευσε τότε.

Heb. xii. 26.

See *Blackwall*'s sacred Classicks, V. i. p. 180.

I.

אַשְׁרֵי הָאִישׁ
אֲשֶׁר לֹא הָלַךְ בַּעֲצַת רְשָׁעִים
וּבְדֶרֶךְ חַטָּאִים לֹא עָמָד
וּבְמוֹשַׁב לֵצִים לֹא יָשָׁב׃

II.

כִּי אִם
בְּתוֹרַת יְהֹוָה חֶפְצוֹ
וּבְתוֹרָתוֹ יֶהְגֶּה
יוֹמָם וָלָיְלָה׃

Now in these Lines the Quantities are so disposed as to constitute the most strong and generous Numbers; which I have distinguished by their proper Marks, and which will more readily appear from the following Resolution of them.

Line
1. Spondee, Iambic.
2. Spondee, Cretic, Anapæst, Bacchic.
3. Choriambic, Bacchic, Cretic.
4. Cretic, Molossus, Cretic.
5. Iambic.
6. Iambic, Cretic, Bacchic.
7. Cretic, Iambic, Anapæst.
8. Spondee, Iambic, Iambic.

When

[41]

When thefe Words are read according to the Quantities here diftinguifhed, the Ear will foon be judge how much more mufical they are than when they are read without any Regard to them. And this Strength of Numbers, together with the Beauty of the Metaphors, and the Elevation of Thought contained in this Sentence, is that which exalts it to a Poetical Character.

The Tranflation of it in Imitation of the fame Profe-Poetical Stile may be in this Manner.

I.

O bleffed Man!

Who walks not in the Councel of the Wicked

Nor in the Way of Sinners ftands,

And in the Seat of Scoffers doth not fit.

II.

But

His Delight is in Jehovah's Law,

In whofe Law he meditates

Day and Night.

II. Of this Kind are moft Monumental Infcriptions, and Panygerick Characters.

Of the former we may take the following Instance.

Hic inhumatur Corpus
MATTHÆI HALE militis;
ROBERTI HALE et JOHANNÆ,
Uxoris ejus, Filii unici
Nati in hâc Parochiâ de *Alderly*,
Primo die Novembris
A. D. 1609.
Denati vero ibidem
Vicesimo quinto die Decembris
A. D. 1676.
Ætatis suæ 67.

Here lies enter'd
The Body of MATTHEW HALE, Knight;
The only Son
Of ROBERT HALE and JOAN his Wife:
Who was born in this Parish of *Alderly*,
On the first Day of November

In the Year of our Lord 1609,

And dy'd in the same Parish,

On the twenty-fifth Day of December,

In the Year of our Lord 1676

Of his Age 67.

Though there is the utmost Simplicity of Words in this Inscription, which Sir *Matthew Hale* ordered to be engraven on his Monument, yet there appears a certain Air of Dignity in them, owing to the Feet that compose them, which are all of the most generous Quality. A plain Instance of the Power of Numbers, even in the most common and simple Language.

And as an Instance of Panygerical Descriptions, which are generally drawn up in this Prose-Poetical Stile, we may take the following Character of the late King *William*.

He was,

But is no more,

The Head, Heart and Hand

Of the Confederacy,

The Assertor of Liberty,

The Deliverer of Nations,
The Support of the *Empire*,
The Bulwark of *Holland*,
The Preserver of *Britain*,
The Reducer of *Ireland*,
And the Terrour of *France*.
His Thoughts were wise, serene and secret,
His Words few and faithful,
His Actions many and heroick;
His Government without Tyranny,
His Justice without Rigour,
And his Religion without Superstition.
He was
Magnanimous without Pride,
Valiant without Violence,
Victorious without Triumph,
Active without Weariness,
Cautious without Fear,
And Meritorious without Thanks.

Though

[45]

Though there be a few weak and faultering Feet in this Panygerick, particularly in the fourth and sixth Lines, yet they are abundantly compenſated by the Energy of Thought, the Succinctneſs of the Language, and the Variety of Contraſt, which makes the Compoſition ſo beautiful. It is not limited to any Feet or Meaſure, and therefore is not Verſe; but is diſtinguiſhed in general by its harmonious Numbers, ſublime Sentiments, with a peculiar terſe, ſtrong and lively Turn of Expreſſion which raiſes it above Proſe, and therefore is a fit Specimen of Proſaic Poetry.

III. Romances and Novels are often writ in this mixt Language, between Poetry and Proſe; and hence it is ſometimes called the *Romantick Stile*. Of which we may take the following Inſtance in the Words of *Alexander* when he took his Leave of *Statira*.——" Madam (ſaid he) I am forced to leave
" you; but though I go from hence, my Thoughts
" ſhall not be ſeperated from you; perhaps I may
" one Day come back to lay all my Victories at
" your Feet; and may the Gods grant, I may be
" as able to conquer your Mind, as I am to con-
" quer Kingdoms; and that I may find you as
" much ſoftened at my Return, as I leave you ob-
" durate at my Departure (*e*)."

(*Laſtly.*)

(*e*) Caſſandra.

(*Lastly.*) Of this Kind also I conceive were the antient *Dithyrambics*; or those Hymns which were formerly sung in Honour of *Bacchus*. Which were a very wild and loose Composition, and as full of Transport and Rage as the drunken God they celebrated. Of these we have no Remains extant: But as *Horace* sais they were tyed to no poetical Numbers (*f*), I take them to be a Species of this Prosaic Poetry.

Before I conclude this Chapter it may not be amiss just to observe the vast Difference between the antient and modern Poetry.

The most antient Poetic Compositions were confined neither to Rhime, Number or Measure; and were nothing but just sublime Sentiments clothed in strong figurative Language. Such was the Oriental Poetry. This was afterward reduced to Measures and Lines; but both very various; the Measures of no determinate Sort, and the Lines of no determinate Length. As in Pindaric Odes. After this the Poetic Stile was bound to still stricter Laws; and confined to a certain Measure, and a certain Number of Feet in every Line, *e. g.* to five dissyllable Feet or ten Syllables; as in *Milton*'s Verse. It was afterwards laid under a further Restriction, and subject not only to Measure but Rhime; and every other Line was to conclude with a Sound similar to that which closed the preceeding Line. And when the Poetry was divided into Stanzas, each Stanza consisting of four Lines of eight and six

---

(*f*) Laureâ donandus Apollinari,
    Seu per audaces nova Dithyrambos
  Verba devolvit, numerisque fertur
    Lege solutis.

Hor. l. iv. Od. 2.

fix Syllables alternately, they were to correfpond in alternate Rhime. And be the Lines ever fo fhort they muft End with a fimilar Sound; and fometimes the two rhiming Syllables are found both in the fame Line; nay according to the Judgment and Tafte of fome People, that is the beft Poetry where the Numbers are leaft varyed and the Rhime moft exact and frequent. Which lays it under the moft miferable Reftraint, hampers it with the moft unreafonable Fetters, cramps a true Poetic Fancy, and whilft it keeps the Attention fixt to the Structure and Sound of Words, takes it off from that which is the very Life and Spirit of all true Poetical Compofition, *viz.* fublime Thought and ftrong Language, it pleafes the Ear at the Expence of our Underftanding, and puts us off with Sound inftead of Senfe.

If the antient Poetry was too lax in its Numbers, the modern is certainly too ftrict. The juft Medium between thefe two Extreams feems to be that which *Milton* hath chofen for his Poem, *viz.* the Penthameter Verfe with the mixt Iambic Meafure, free from the Shackle of Rhime; in which the Numbers are neither too free nor too confined; but are mufical enough to entertain the Ear, and at the fame Time leave Room enough to exprefs the ftrongeft Thought in the beft and boldeft Language.

CHAP.

CHAP. VIII.

The Composition of some of our best English Writers considered with Regard to their Numbers.

ARCHBISHOP *Sharp*, whose Sermons for Perspicuity of Stile, Solidity of Sense, and Piety of Spirit, are deservedly admired, was nevertheless very negligent of his Rhythmus. We are frequently hampered with four or five short Syllables together, *e. g.* " This I must confess is a very

" melancholy and unpleasing Argument (*g*)." Which he might with Ease have prevented, only by putting the Word *Unpleasing* first. Again, " We are not

" much degenerated from the Purity of Christianity

" as to Doctrinals (*h*)." And what is worse, he often closes with a double Pyrrhic. *e. g.* " I speak
" of the national Sins, the reigning Vices of the

" Times, the Miscarriages that are so prevailing and
" so common that a Publick Guilt is contracted
" by them, and the whole People may justly share

" in the Punishment of them (*i*)."

Arch-

(*g*) Vol ii. p. 6.
(*h*) Ibid.
(*i*) Id. p. 7.

Archbishop *Tillotson* hath all the Simplicity and Perspicuity of the former, but is much more harmonious. He had a nice Ear and a clear Head; was happy in the Sweetness of his Numbers, an inimitable Ease of Stile and Solidity of Argument. For these he hath been ever admired, and one unharmonious Sentence picked out of three Volumes in Folio, I believe will not be deemed Proof sufficient to overthrow so well established a Reputation. And therefore I cannot help thinking that the Censure lately passed upon him by a very elegant Writer is somewhat too severe (*k*). If the Archbishop (whom no Man of Taste can read without Pleasure) be defective in any Thing, it is in Force and Spirit, and when this seems to be most wanting, it is oftentimes only concealed by a peculiar Simplicity of Language. Let us take the following Passage for an Instance,——" But of all Doctrines in the World,
" it (*i. e.* the Doctrine of Transubstantiation) is pe-
" culiarly incapable of being proved by a Miracle.
" For if a Miracle were wrought for the Proof of
" it, the very same Assurance which a Man hath
" of the Truth of the Miracle, he hath of the
" Falshood of the Doctrine, that is, the clear Evi-
" dence

(*k*) See *Fitzosborn*'s Letters, Let. xxiv.
It is without Doubt altogether as wrong to condemn a good Composition for here and there a rough Period, as it is to applaud a bad Composition for here and there a good one. No Man, I believe, will dispute the late Lord B——*k*'s Claim to the Rank of a fine Writer; yet even his Stile is not always free from ill-turned Periods and a bad Disposition of Numbers. —— *By never saying what is unfit for him to say, he will never hear what is unfit for him to bear; by never doing what is unfit for him to do, he will never see what is unfit for him to see.*—— Again, *If the Heart of a Prince be not corrupt, these Truths will find an easy Ingression through the Understanding to it.* Letters on the Spirit of Patriotism, &c. p. 218, 223.——Who does not see that the former of these Periods has too much of the low affected Turn and Jingle of the last Century to please in this; and that the closing Numbers in the latter are halting, weak and unharmonious.

[50]

"dence of his Senses for both. For that there is
a Miracle wrought to prove, *that what he sees
in the Sacrament is not Bread, but the Body of
Christ*, he hath only the Evidence of his Senses:
And he hath the very same Evidence to prove,
*that what he sees in the Sacrament is not the
Body of Christ, but Bread.* So that the Argument for Transubstantiation, and the Objection
against it, do just ballance one another; and
where the Weights in both Scales are equal, it
is impossible that the one should weigh down
the other; and consequently Transubstantiation
is not to be proved by a Miracle; for that would
be, *to prove to a Man by something that he sees,
that he does not see what he sees* (*l*)."

Never was there a more perfect Master of Numbers, both in Poetry and Prose, than Mr. *Addison.* *Fair Rosamond* will always be a Proof of the one, and his *Spectators* a lasting Monument of the other. It is no less needless than it would be endless to specify the particular Beauties of his Language, which at once excels in Purity, Perspicuity and Force; and in which it is equally difficult to find either Defect or Redundance. In a Word, the best Way to acquire a chaste, expressive and numerous Stile is to read and copy him.

Mr. G⸺n is full of Force and Fire; his Stile nervous and pointed; well turned for Raillery, and far above the common Level. His Numbers most strong and generous; happily adapted to please the Ear and reach the Heart. He hath *Seneca*'s Point without his Poverty, *Tully*'s Spirit without his Profuseness,

(*l*) *Tillotson*'s Works, Vol. i. p. 179. Serm. 21.

fufenefs, and *Demofthenes*'s Thunder without his Lightning. For a Specimen we may take the following Paragraph; where speaking of the formidable Tribe of Critics, he fais thus,—" The common
" Fraternity of Writers (a moft *unbrotherly* Fra-
" ternity) furnifh a Swarm of Critics. For almoft
" all Writers are Critics in the rigorous, but wrong
" Senfe of the Word; and are therefore ready to
" run down all fuperior Productions; and to fhew
" the leaft Mercy to the moft Merit. If any Work
" merit Praife, this is to them fufficient Provocation to
" decry it. I have known fome of them appear fond
" of a Book, till they faw it fucceed, then grow
" mad at its Succefs, and wondered at the foolifh
" Tafte of the Town. As I have received many
" Proofs of their good-will, I know their Candour.
" I have found fome fo vain, that no good Treat-
" ment could reach their Merit, fome fo craving
" as only to be beholden for Favours to come; o-
" thers who have praifed me too copioufly without
" any Court or Temptation from me, have
" abufed me as plentifully without being once
" offended by me: Others, fo little Scrupulous as
" to revile me for Writings which I never wrote. I
" can produce as high a Panegyric as ever was made
" upon Man, and as vile a Libel, both in Print, and
" both from the fame Author; the former without
" my ever having feen him, and the latter without
" ever having wronged him; nay, after I had done
" him a thoufand good Offices. I have fupported an
" Author for a whole Winter, and have had his Thanks
" next Summer in a furious printed Invective (*m*)."

(*m*) See Introduction to a Tranflation of *Salluft*, p. 18, 19.

My Lord *Shaftſbury*'s Numbers, if compared with the two Authors laſt mentioned, are not ſo ſweet as thoſe of the firſt, nor ſo ſtrong as thoſe of the laſt. His Talent is delicate Ridicule, but his Stile not very fit for it; which is rather weak and fluent than harmoniouſly ſtrong. He wears a perpetual Face of Pleaſantry, and loves to laugh; but has ſometimes the Misfortune to laugh out of Seaſon, and draw the Smile upon himſelf. His Expreſſions are now and then no leſs Quaint than his Humour; but the Numbers of the former as ill-matched as the Subjects of the latter. However he hath gained the Character of a fine Author, which I apprehend he owes more to the Dignity of his Name, than that of his Writings. He affects Delicacy, but does not always preſerve it. Of which the following Lines are a Proof.—" It is obſervable that the

" Writers of *Memoirs* and *Eſſays* are chiefly Sub-
" ject to this *frothy* Diſtemper. Nor can it be
" doubted that this is the true Reaſon why theſe

" Gentlemen entertain the World ſo laviſhly with

" what relates to themſelves. Who indeed can
" endure to hear an Emperick talk of his own Con-

" ſtitution, how he governs and manages it, what
" Diet agrees beſt with it, and what his Practice
" *is with himſelf.* The Proverb, no doubt, is very
" juſt, *Phyſician cure thyſelf.* Yet methinks one
" ſhould have but an ill Time, to be preſent at

" theſe *bodily Operations.* Nor is the Reader in
" Truth *any* better entertained, when he is obliged
" to aſſiſt at the *experimental Diſcuſſions* of his *practi-*
" *ſing*

" *fing* Author, who all the while is in reality doing no
" better than *taking his Phyfick in Publick* (*n*)."

Bifhop *Atterbury* was doubtlefs a great Genius, and a fine Writer. No one difputes his Claim to Eloquence. His Numbers are well chofen, beautiful and ftrong as the Senfe they convey; his Expreffion pure, his Cadence fmooth, his Phrafe eafy, and his Clofes full of Harmony. As a Specimen of which, take the following Extract from a Letter of his to Mr. *Pope*.—" I thank you for a Sight
" of your Verfes; and with the Freedom of an
" honeft, though perhaps injudicious Friend, muft
" tell you; that though I could like fome of them
" if they were any Body's elfe but yours, yet as
" they are yours, and to be owned as fuch, I
" can fcarce like any of them. Not but that the
" four firft Lines are good, efpecially the fecond
" Couplet; and might if followed by four others
" as good, give Reputation to a Writer of a lefs
" eftablifhed Fame. But from you I expect fome-
" thing of a more perfect Kind, and which, the
" oftener it is read, the more it will be admired.
" When you barely exceed other Writers, you fall
" much beneath yourfelf (*o*).

Having

(*n*) See Characterifticks, Vol. i. p. 163.
(*o*) See Letters to and from Dr. *Atterbury* Bifhop of *Rochefter*, Lett. 24.

Having mentioned Mr. *Pope*, I muſt produce him next. He would have ſhone no leſs in Proſe than Poetry, had he applyed himſelf as much to the former as he did to the latter. This appears from his Letters; where you ſee nothing of the Poet, none of thoſe fanciful Images or excurſive Flights, ſo natural to thoſe who have dealt much in Verſe; but all is ſmooth eaſy Language, ſtrong and ſolid Senſe. His Numbers are purely Proſaic, but flow with a Sweetneſs peculiar to one whoſe Soul was all Harmony. Writing to his Friend, the forementioned Biſhop, when under Diſgrace, he ſais—" Once
" more I write to you as I promiſed; and this once
" I fear will be the laſt! The Curtain will ſoon be
" drawn between my Friend and me, and nothing
" left but to wiſh you a long good Night.—If you
" retain any Memory of the paſt, let it only Image
" to you what hath pleaſed you beſt; ſometimes
" preſent a Dream of an abſent Friend, or bring
" you back an agreeable Converſation. But upon
" the whole, I hope you will think leſs of the Time
" paſt, than the future; as the former hath been
" leſs kind to you than the latter infallibly will be.
" Do not envy the World your Studies; they will
" tend to the Benefit of Men againſt whom you

can

"can have no Complaint; I mean of all Posterity. And perhaps at your Time of Life, nothing else is worth your Care. What is every Year of a wise Man's Life, but a Censure or Critique on the past? Those whose Date is shortest, live long enough to laugh at one half of it. The Boy despises the Infant, the Man the Boy, the Philosopher both, and the Christian all (*p*)."

I have marked the Closes, that the Reader may observe the Numbers to which they owe their Sweetness.

I should tire my Readers and myself, were I to mention half our English Authors whose Writings have done an Honour to our Language, and who owe their Fame for Eloquence chiefly to their Skill in Numbers. But it would justly be deemed a want of Taste or Memory, not to mention in this Number the excellent Mr. M⸺th; who hath lately obliged the World with a Collection of Letters full of fine Sense and fine Language. All the Spirit, Ease and Elegance of original Epistles enter into his Translation of *Pliny*'s: Where the Reader is at once charmed with a Beauty of Thought and Diction, scarce to be paralleled by any but those of *Fitzosborn*. Taking Occasion from a Passage in *Pliny* to recommend Epistolary Writing, he sais, —" It

(*p*) Id. Letter xxiii.

—" It appears from this and some other Passages
" in those Letters, that the Art of Epistolary Wri-
" ing was esteemed by the Romans, in the Num-
" ber of liberal and polite Accomplishments. It
" seems indeed to have formed Part of their Educa-
" tion; as in the Opinion of Mr. *Lock* it well de-
" serves to have a Share in ours.——It is to be won-
" dered that we have so few Writers in our own
" Language, who deserve to be pointed out as Mo-
" dels upon such an Occasion.—A late distinguish-
" ed Genius treats the very Attempt as ridiculous,
" and professes himself *a mortal Enemy to what*
" *they call a fine Letter.* His Aversion however
" was not so strong but he knew how to conquer
" it when he thought proper; and the Letter which
" closes his Correspondence with Bishop *Atterbu-*
" *ry* (*q*), is perhaps the most genteel and manly Ad-
" dress that was ever pen'd to a Friend in Dis-
" grace (*r*)."

A nice

(*q*) Referring to the Letter out of which I have taken the Extract above
(*r*) See *Pliny*'s Letters, B. 2. Let. 13. not. (*a*).

A nice Ear will soon perceive a Difference in the Stile of the two last mentioned Writers. They are both numerous, both harmonious, but in a different Way. The First is more Succinct and Nervous, the Latter more Diffuse and Flowing. And a judicious Reader will as soon discern the Cause to which this Difference is owing, *viz.* because the one deals most in Spondaic and Iambic, the other in Dactylic and Anapæstic Numbers.

I must not omit here to mention Mr. *Smith*; who (if I mistake not) hath translated *Longinus* in the true *Sublime:* And seems as much inspired by the Spirit of his Author, as his Author himself was by the Nature of his Subject: And both were a happy Specimen of the Art they taught. And though he speaks in very diminutive Terms of the Rules the Antients laid down to attain a numerous Composition (which he owns *Cicero* study'd and practised (*s*)) and apprehends they will throw too great a Restraint and Incumbrance on our Language, yet his own Stile is, I think, a Proof of the Contrary. For whatever Aversion he might have to the Rules of this Art, he knew how to practise them with very good Success. For condoling the Publick on the Loss they have sustained by that of *Longinus*'s Treatise on the Passions, he sais,—" the Excellence

" of this on the *Sublime* makes us regret the more
" the Loss of the other; and inspires us with a deep
" Resentment of the irreparable Depredations com-
" mitted on Learning and the valuable Productions
" of Antiquity, by *Goths*, and Monks, and Time.
" There

(*s*) See his Notes and Observations on *Longinus*, Sect. 39.

"There, in all Probability we should have beheld
"the secret Springs and Movements of the Soul
"disclosed to View. There, we should have been
"taught, if Rule and Observation in this Case can
"teach, to elevate an Audience into Joy, or melt
"them into Tears. There, we should have learn'd
"if ever, to work upon every Passion, to put every
"Heart, every Pulse in Emotion. At present we
"must sit down contented under the Loss, and be
"satisfyed with this invaluable Piece on the Sublime,
"which with much Hazard hath escaped a Wreck,
"and gain'd a Port though not undamag'd (*t*)."

Sir *William Temple*'s nervous and masculine Stile is a good deal owing to the strong, majestick Numbers of his Composition.—" To find any Felicity,
"or take any Pleasure in the greatest Advantages of
"Honour and Fortune, a Man must be in Health.
"Who would not be Covetous, and with Reason,
"if this could be purchased with Gold? Who not
"Ambitious, if it were at the Command of Power,
"or restored by Honour. But alas! A white Staff
will

(*t*) Notes and Observations on *Longinus*, ad fin.

[59]

" will not help gouty Feet to walk, better than a
" common Cane; nor a blue Ribband bind up a
" Wound so well as a Fillet. The glitter of Gold
" or of Diamonds will but hurt sore Eyes, instead
" of curing them. And an aking Head will be no
" more eased by wearing a Crown, than a com-
" mon Night-Cap (*u*)."

I know not how to conclude this Chapter without observing, that the Translators of our English Bible are usually very happy in their Numbers; which are mostly solemn, majestic and grave as the sacred Subjects they treat of. For an Instance, let us take the four first Verses of Saint *John*'s Gospel.

" In the Be|ginning was| the Word, | and the
" Word | was with God, | and the Word | was God.

" The same | was in the | Begin|ning with God.

" All Things were | made by him, | and without
" him was | not a|ny Thing made | that was made.

" In him | was Life, | and the Life | was the Light |
" of Man."

(*u*) See his Miscellanies, Part iii. p. 110:
To the forementioned Writers eminent for numerous Composition I might justly add, Dr. *Middleton*, Dr. *Burnet*, Mr. *Geddes*, Mr. *Baiguy*, Mr. *Grove*, Dr. *Watts*, and Mr. *Hervey*. But the Language of the two last, is, for the most Part, too Poetical.

A Man muſt have no Ear, no Taſte, that does not perceive in this Paragraph, with how much Harmony the Subject and Numbers accord. And perhaps there is no Paſſage in any Writings ſacred or profane, that exceeds it in Sublimity of Sentiment and Dignity of Diction.

By this Time, I hope we have a diſtinct Idea of what is generally called a *numerous Compoſition*. It hath no reference to a Writer's Sentiments: For good Thoughts may be, and very often are, expreſſed in a very bad Manner. It does not refer to the Propriety of Expreſſion: For the propereſt Words are ſometimes harſh and diſcordant; and Nonſenſe may be muſical. Nor is a numerous Stile only a ſmooth flowing Stile, as ſome imagine, but an harmonious and muſical Stile. Or ſuch an Arrangement and Diſpoſition of the Words, as gives the Ear a Pleaſure when they are pronounced. The Sound of the Hautboy and Trumpet is muſical as well as that of the Harp and Lute: But the Muſick of the one is loud and ſtrong, that of the other ſoft and ſweet. For there is as great a Diverſity in muſical Numbers, as there is in muſical Notes; and as great a Variety of Harmony ariſing from the different Diſpoſition of them: So *G—n* and *Temple* are excellent for numerous Compoſition as well as *Tillotſon* and *M——th*: But the Numbers of the former are more maſculine and ſtrong, thoſe of the latter more ſoft and flowing; both equally Harmonious.

And from hence alſo we may obſerve not only a great Difference in the Stile or Compoſition of Writers, but the Cauſe of that Difference. The
ſoft

soft and flowing Stile arises from the great Number of short Quantities or rapid Feet, and the strong and masculine Stile from the long Quantities and grave Numbers which compose it. For it is the Numbers with which the Periods and the several Parts of them close, that gives the particular Distinction and Air to the Structure of the Sentence. And according to these an Author may be said (in Prose as well as Verse) to write in the *Dactylic* or *Iambic* Measure; *i. e.* according as he closes most frequently with Dactyles or Iambics: (so *Tully* sais that *Ephormus* the Orator followed the Dactylic (*x*) Measure) For every Author naturally runs into one of these different Measures more than the other; as he does into the Use of some particular Words and Phrases: And these two Things (though the former is not so often observed as the latter) are the Cause that a Man is no less distinguished by his Stile than his Hand-Writing.

CHAP. IX.

Containing certain Rules proper to be observed in Order to acquire a numerous Stile.

Rule I. FURNISH yourself with a Copia of equivalent Words, or Words that convey just the same Idea; that you may have it in your Power to substitute one of a good Number in the

(*x*) *Orator*, p. 166. (a).

the Room of another that is a bad one, and to chuse that which best suits the Rhythmus, of which a good Ear will soon be Judge.

This Rule *Quintilian* sais was observed by some in his Time, who for this Purpose got a Store of such Words by Heart (*y*). But he observes that such a Furniture is best provided by a careful Attention to the Manner of Speaking and Writing used by the best Masters of Language; because by this Means we shall know not only the best Words but their best Situation (*z*). And of two Words equally proper and expressive, that which contains the best Number is for the most Part to be prefered.

Rule II. When four, five, or more short Syllables come together, you may Part them by inserting amongst them some expletive Particle containing a long Quantity; which if it do not strengthen the Sense, will at least serve to meliorate the Measure.

Take for Example the following Sentence; *This Doctrine I apprehend to be erroneous and of a pernicious Tendency.* Here too many short Quantities follow one another successively. But suppose it altered thus; *This Doctrine I take to be not only false, but of very pernicious Tendency*; and let any good Ear judge to which the Preference is due.

The same Thing may be done in Order to prevent the Collision of two hard Sounds, which (tho' the

---

(*y*) Equidem scio quosdam collecta quæ Idem significarent Vocabula solitos ediscere, quo facilius occurreret unum ex pluribus. l. x. c. 1.
(*z*) Ibid.

the Number be good yet) require some Pains to be distinctly pronounced, without grating on the Ear. For this Reason the Translators of the New Testament render the Words in *Luke* x. 11. thus; *even the very Dust of your City which cleaveth on us, we* DO *wipe off against you.* Not *we wipe*; which are Sounds so ready to run into one another, that they require some Care and Pause to keep them asunder (*a*).

Rule III. An *Illipsis* will often help the Rhythmus, by contracting two Syllables into one, as *'tis, don't*; for *it is, do not*.

And to mend the Measure we may often leave out not only some Syllables in a Word, but some whole Words in a Sentence, provided we do not thereby weaken or obscure the Sense. So the Adverb *that*, and the Particle *the*, may be either expressed or understood, according as it best suits the Run of the Words. *e. g.* I see *that* nothing can be done to save either *the* Man or *the* Horse. Better thus, *I see nothing can be done to save either Man or Horse.*

Nay, for the same End an Author may drop, not only a whole Word, but Part of a Period, and leave the Sense imperfect in some obvious Cases. And a seasonable Silence, or imperfect Speech (a Figure which the Rhetoricians (*b*) call a *Suppression*) often serves at once to strengthen both the Measure and Sentiment. As in that Expression in *Terence, Liber Loris!*—" To cause a Period then to
" run with a greater Smoothness and just Cadency,
" an Author will find himself obliged, not only
" to

(*a*) *Say*'s Essay on Numbers, &c. p. 115.
(*b*) *Blackwall*'s Introduction to the Classicks, p. 185.

"to ſtrip it of all Superfluities, but even to leave out ſomething in the Senſe, which the Reader muſt neceſſarily ſupply from his own Invention. *Demoſthenes*, but eſpecially *Thucydides*, abound with Inſtances of this. Nor is a Reader of Taſte at all offended with it; on the Contrary he is pleaſed with the Compliment paid his Underſtanding (*c*)."—Theſe laſt Words exemplify the Rule we are upon; and run much better as they are, than if they had been—" He is pleaſed with the Compliment *which is* paid *to* his Underſtanding."

Rule IV. A proper Uſe of Rhetorical Figures is ſometimes a great Help to a numerous Compoſition; and when they are well choſen and pertinently applied, they ſerve at once to exalt the Senſe and adorn the Language (*d*).

But here the following Things muſt be carefully remembered.

(1.) That the Figures we Uſe be neither obſcure nor impertinent. Which will only darken or perplex the Senſe (*e*).

(2.) That they be not too bold and ſtrong. For that favours too much of Poetry.

(3.) That they be not ſtiff or unnatural. Which diſcovers a ridiculous Affectation.

(4.) That

(*c*) *Geddes* on Compoſition, p. 5.

(*d*) Sed et figuris mutare et caſus et numeros, quorum Varietas frequenter gratia Compoſitionis adſtricta, etiam ſine numero ſolet eſſe jucunda. *Quintil* l. ix. c. 4.

(*e*) See *Fitzoſborne's* Letters. Let 51.

(4.) That they be not too frequent. Because that will tire and surfeit the Reader; who does not love to have more Sauſe than Meat.

This was Mr. *Cowley*'s great Fault, who runs us quite down with his Rhetorical Wit, and gives us no Time to breathe (*f*).

(5.) That they be introduced ſuddenly without any previous Form or Notice. For nothing is more agreeable than to be *ſurpriſed* with Pleaſure. And when ſuch figurative Forms of Speech give a Harmony to the Stile (as they often do) the Pleaſure is ſtill augmented.

Rule V. A Tranſpoſition of Words is very frequently uſed for the Sake of a good Rhythm and emphatical Cloſe.

(*d*) Speaking of a Perſon who had publiſhed a Paltry Poem in his Name, he purſues him with the following exquiſite Raillery. ———
" I wondered very much how one who could be ſo fooliſh to write ſo
" ill Verſes, ſhould be ſo wiſe to ſet them forth as *another Man's*
" rather than *his own*; though perhaps he might have made a better
" Choice, and not fathered the *Baſtard* upon ſuch a Perſon, whoſe
" Stock of Reputation is, I fear, little enough for Maintenance of his
" own numerous *Legitimate* Offspring of that Kind. It would have
" been much leſs injurious, if it had pleaſed the Author, to put forth
" ſome of my Writings under his *own name*, rather than his own un-
" der *mine*. He had been in that a more pardonable Plagiary, and
" had done leſs wrong by *Robbery*, than he does by ſuch a *Bounty*.
" —— Our own *coarſe Clothes* are like to become us better than thoſe of
" another Man's, though never ſo *rich*. But theſe; to ſay the Truth,
" were ſo *beggarly*, that I myſelf was aſhamed to wear them. It was
" in vain for me that I avoided cenſure by the Concealment of my
" own Writings, if my Reputation could be thus *executed in Effigy*.
" And impoſſible it is for any good name to be in ſafety, if the ma-
" lice of Witches have the Power to conſume and deſtroy it in an I-
" mage of their own making This indeed was ſo ill made, and ſo
" *unlike*, that I hope the *Charm* took no effect."
Preface to his Poems.

This is the true Reason that we find such a Change of the natural Order of Words so common in all Languages, especially in the *Latin*; and in the best Writers, especially in *Cicero*: Who often postpones to the very last, that Verb or emphatical Word on which the whole Sense of the Period depends.

But two Things are observable in him, in which he ought to be imitated, *viz.*

(1.) He does not leave the Mind in the mean Time altogether at a Loss for the general Sense, but so disposes of the intermediate Words, that we may readily guess at his Meaning before it be fully expressed.

(2.) When the long looked for Word is come, it is generally more elegant and emphatical than even the Mind or the Ear, so long suspended could expect; and throws such a sudden and surprising Light and Beauty upon the whole, as more than compensates the Pain of that Suspence.

Instances of this are obvious and numberless. Without the former, the Sense would be obscured; and without the latter, the Mind would suffer a Disappointment, which no Harmony or Close could recompence.

Therefore

Rule VI. Let the Sentence always close, if possible, not only with a good Number, but an emphatical Word.

By which I don't mean that the emphatical Word must of Necessity be the very last: If it be within three or four Syllables of it, it may do as well,

and

and be confidered as the Clofe. Nor are the Words for the Sake of this Elegance to be unnaturally tranſpoſed, ſo as to darken the Senſe or ſpoil the other Numbers: But you ſhould keep it in View, and when it is natural nothing is more beautiful.

To this may be added another Thing which bears ſome Reſemblance to it, *viz.* To cloſe with a Word that ſtands in a lively Reference or Contraſt to ſome other in the ſame Sentence.—This will always be agreeable, eſpecially if both Words be Emphatical. *e. g.* " Unhappy Man, who obtaining the *Pleaſure* " he ſo long purſued, finds himſelf at laſt poſſeſſed " of *Pain!* "

Rule VII. Remark the moſt beautiful Cloſes, as well as the propereſt Words, in the Writings and Converſation of thoſe who moſt excel in Elegance of Stile.

In this Reſpect you will reap great Advantage from a good Acquaintance with the Authors before mentioned, and many others that are equally excellent in the ſame Way. Becauſe, as *Quintilian* takes Notice (g), you will there obſerve not only the beſt Words but their beſt Places; for a good Word miſplaced ſpoils the Harmony as much as a good Word miſapplyed does the Senſe.

And ſince there is a great Diverſity in the Stile, of good Writers, ſome being more copious and flowing, and others more conciſe and nervous, be moſt converſant with what you like beſt; becauſe *that* you will be moſt apt to imitate. Nor ſhould you deal much in thoſe Authors who are quite negligent of their Rhythm, unleſs the Importance of the

(g) L. x. c. 1.

Senſe compenſate the Want of Harmony; for if you have a good Ear they will diſguſt you; and if none, will betray you into an imitation of their rugged Stile, which will diſguſt others.

And when you have gained a Competent Knowledge of the Rhythmical Theory, it will be pleaſant to obſerve how naturally a good Ear leads the moſt illiterate Perſons in their common Speech to the Choice of the beſt Numbers, who are intirely ignorant of all the Rules and Principles of numerous Compoſition; and how plainly Nature exemplifys thoſe Rules which were originally invented for the Imitation of it.

Rule VIII. Let your firſt Care be a clear and ſtrong Expreſſion of the Sentiment; what is rough and harſh in the Numbers may be rectifyed afterwards.

But never change a proper, ſtrong, expreſſive Word that is unharmonious, for one that does not convey the Idea ſo fully though it contains a better Number. For this Reaſon, becauſe Senſe is always to be prefered to Sound, and the Mind to be entertained before the Ear (*h*). And ſpecial Care muſt be taken that a too ſcrupulous Attention to the ſmooth Flow of the Period do not render the Senſe confuſed or the Stile enervate.

Rule IX. Do not uſe always the ſame Sort of Numbers, be they ever ſo good; the Ear will ſoon perceive the Uniformity and be offended at it (*i*).

You

(*h*) In univerſum autem, ſi ſit neceſſe, duram potius atque aſperam compoſitionem malim eſſe, quam effeminatam et enervem, qualis apud multos.—— Et certe nullum aptum et idoneum Verbum permutemus gratia lenitatis. *Quint.* l. IX. c. 4. ad finem.

(*i*) Ac ne tam bona quidem ulla erit, ut debeat eſſe continua, et in eodem ſemper pedes ire. Nam et verſificandi genus eſt, unam legem omnibus

You should endeavour not only to introduce the beſt Numbers, but thoſe that beſt ſuit the Subject they deſcribe; and vary them as that varies. *e. g.* Grave and ſolemn Subjects ſhould move in ſlow and ſtately *Spondees*; Paſſions run off quick in *Pyrrhic*; what is ſtrong and alarming is beſt expreſſed in *Iambic*, and what is ſoft and tender in *Trochaic* Meaſure: For a conſtant Uniformity of Meaſure, though ever ſo ſweet and fluent, ſatiates and tires the Ear. This is no leſs true in Proſaic than Poetic Compoſition.

Rule X. Let your Compoſition be ſo free, natural, and eaſy, that you may not ſeem to have any Regard to your Numbers at all.

The foregoing Rules you ſhould carefully follow, but the Reader muſt not obſerve that you do ſo. This Art of all others, requires the greateſt Art to conceal it. An Orator will certainly miſs of his Aim if his Hearers once ſuſpect, that by bribing their Ears he means to make his Way to their Hearts (*k*).

As Art is an Imitation of Nature, *that* is the moſt perfect Art which reſembles Nature moſt. And what is unnatural, be it ever ſo much laboured will have no Power either to pleaſe or perſwade. And ſometimes it requires the greateſt Labour not to ſeem elaborate (*l*).

Theſe
omnibus Sermonibus dare: et id cum manifeſta Affectatio eſt (cujus rei maxime cavenda ſuſpicio eſt) tum etiam ſimilitudine tædium ac ſatietatem creat. *Ibid.*

(*k*) Amittitque et fidem et affectus motuſque omnes qui eſt in hac cura deprehenſus: nec poteſt ei credere aut propter eum dolere et iraſci Judex, cui putat hoc vacare *Quint.* l. ix. c. 4. ad finem.

(*l*) Illa quidem maximi laboris, ne laborata videantur.—Diſſimulatio Curæ præcipua, ut numeri ſponte fluxiſſe, non arceſſiti et coacti eſſe videantur. *Ibid.*

These are some of the principal Rules which regard a numerous Composition: To which it may not be amiss briefly to adjoin a few others of a more general Nature; which though they do not immediately relate to Numbers, and perhaps may appear too minute to some, yet I am perswaded will be of Service (especially to young Students) in the Art of Composing, so far as it regards the Language.

(1.) Two long Sentences should not stand together, though many short ones may.

The Reason of this is plain. Because the former require too great Expense of Breath to pronounce them, and too much Intenseness of Thought to comprehend the full Sense of them; which the latter doe not. And a Writer should always have a Regard to the Ease of his Readers (*m*). It is a vile Affectation in an Author, lest he should not appear learned, to be afraid of making Things too plain. A long Period therefore is better divided into two short ones, containing just the same Sense, if it conveniently may.

(2.) Words

(*m*) " When the Reader is greatly perplexed and at a Loss for the Meaning, though the Diction be ever so elegant, the Charm vanishes. The Musick is drowned amidst the Hurry and Confusion of Sentiments. It seems a just Rule in Polite Writing, though not always observed by the Moderns, that two long Sentences ought never successively to follow one another. Seldom, if ever, will you find either in *Demosthenes* or *Plato*, any remarkable Deviation from this Rule. They were too good Judges in Composition, not to know that a Repetition of the same Length of Period becomes flat and insipid. The dwelling too long on one Note is offensive to the Ear. Whereas if you intermingle a *laconic* Conciseness, and frequently introduce short, nervous, clear, expressive Sentences, after one greatly prolonged, the Effect such a Method has on the Mind is wonderful, the Variety extreamly entertaining." *Geddes* on Composition, p. 6.

(2.) Words of fimilar Sound or Terminations fhould be avoided, or at leaft be kept at a good Diftance the one from the other. For if they are fo near together as to' jingle in the Ear, they will certainly offend it.

(3.) The Concurrence of many *Genitives* with their Sign *of* prefixed, fhould be avoided as an inelegance. Two may fometimes be admitted, but three never. *e. g. I have thrown off moft of my Sufpicions of the Sincerity of your Intentions.*

(4.) That which fome call *Alliteration, i. e.* beginning feveral Words with the fame Letter, if it be natural, is a real Beauty, and not to be defpifed; and accordingly we find it practifed by fome of the beft Authors; particularly Mr. *Pope.*

But here we muft except againft two Letters, *viz.* (*w*) and (*s*). The firft becaufe there is fome difficulty in the Formation of its Sound; and therefore when two Words meet which begin with it, they had better be feparated by fome expletive Particle, to which a good Ear will readily direct.—— The fame may be faid of (*th*).

And the frequent Concurrence of the (*s*) muft be avoided, becaufe it creates a difagreeable Hiffing in the Voice; a Fault which Foreigners univerfally find in our Language: and is occafioned by three Letters in the Englifh Alphabet which convey that Sound, *viz.* (*s*), (*z*) and foft (*c*): And we ftill increafe it by an Affectation of changing the Termination *eth* into *es, e. g. bears, loves, does,* for *beareth, loveth, doeth.*

(5.) Do not often conclude a Sentence with the Sign of the *Genetive* or *Ablative* Case; because that precludes an Elegance you should always aim at, *viz.* closing with an emphatical Word. e. g. *Perfect Vertue is the highest Happiness Mankind are capable of, and Reason the Rule they are to walk by.* Better thus, *Perfect Vertue is the highest Happiness of which Mankind are capable, and Reason the Rule by which they are to walk.*——But the other Close is not to be universally rejected, and a good Rhythm will determine which of them we ought to chuse.

(6.) When a Word ends with a Vowel distinctly heard, the following Word should not begin with the same if it may conveniently be avoided; much less with a Syllable of the like Sound. *e. g.* " Ano*ther* " *there*fore may make a *due Use* of the Command- " *ment* men*t*ioned in every regard." What Ear can bear to be thus grated!

CHAP. X.

The Advantage of a numerous Composition.

THE first Question a wise Man will put to himself in any considerable Affair or Business he undertakes, is, *cui Bono?* What good End will it answer? And is the Benefit expected from it equal to the Pains it requires? If not, it will be in Part *Labour in vain*; a serious Trifling; and spending Time *laboriose nihil agendo.* An Imputation, of which perhaps some may suppose the Writer of these Essays

does

does not stand altogether clear, and from which he is very desirous, if possible, to be absolved.

I have, it is true, been leading the Reader in a Path which of late hath been little frequented; and having conducted him through it, I am now to inform him for what Reason I have brought him hither. For it may justly be asked, If it be a Way worth pursuing, why has it lain so long neglected? If not, what need of all this Pains to clear it?— To which the Answer is ready. It is a Way worth pursuing; and the Reason why this Science (to dismiss the Metaphor) hath been so long neglected, is owing in Part to the Difficulty of reducing it to any certain just Rules and Principles which may discover the Foundation of it, and give the Mind a right Direction in it; and in Part to an Ignorance of the great Advantage which flows from a good Acquaintance with it. The former I have endeavoured to investigate and explain in the preceeding Chapters, and the latter I am briefly to specify in this, that the Reader may not look upon all his Labour as lost.

And in the first Place, a familiar Acquaintance with the Rules and Principles of Prosaic Numbers will contribute a good deal to the Facility of Composition. When a Person by a little Care and Practice is once Master of a neat and numerous Stile, he will find it no longer difficult to express his best Sentiments in a lively Manner; if his Conceptions be clear, his Stile will be so too; and will discover the Spirit of true Oratory without the Pomp of it.

And in revising his Composures he will be able to correct them with more Judgment; and when he discerns a Roughness or Lameness in his Stile, which his Ear may discover, he will immediately perceive the beſt Way to correct and ſmooth it; wherein he will find but little Aſſiſtance from the Ear alone, which in this Caſe is a better Judge than Guide.

Beſides, a good Skill in the Principles of numerical Structure opens to us one chief Source of that Pleaſure which in the Stile of a well-compoſed Piece, we have often taſted, but never knew before from whence it ſprung; which cannot fail to give an agreeable Entertainment to a curious and inquiſitive Mind, which not content with a Set of formal Notions, wants to ſurvey their Foundation and trace them up to their firſt Principles. And will teach us to judge better not only of our own Compoſitions but thoſe of other Men; and will at once enlarge our View and improve our Taſte of Books and Language.

When we are once well verſed in this Science, it will be no ſmall Help to our Expreſſion, even on common Occaſions, and give a graceful Turn to our Language in ordinary Diſcourſe. It's a pleaſing Amuſement, in which I have often indulged myſelf, to obſerve how naturally Men run into thoſe Numbers in vulgar Stile, which are beſt adapted to the Spirit of the Subject they talk of, or the Paſſions which animate the Perſon that ſpeaks; and which to a curious Obſerver are diſtinguiſhable no leſs by the Numbers of his Stile than the Tone of his Voice. Thus, Reſentment and Wrath are expreſſed not only with a loud and boiſterous Tone, but in bold and daring Numbers; whereas in Sorrow, Complaint and Pity, the Numbers, like the Voice, are low, feeble, flexible and faultering. And almoſt all the foregoing Rules you may obſerve, with a little Attention, to be clearly exemplify'd in the Dialect of the moſt illiterate Perſons. For however defective they be in a Propriety

of

of Expreſſion, they are generally very happy in their Rhythmus; to which they are directed by the Ear, or the natural Harmony of Sounds. In a particular Manner you may obſerve the Beauty of their Cloſes; for they commonly finiſh their Periods with Anapæſtics or Iambics (*Ariſtotle* faith (*n*), chiefly with Iambics) and very frequently with an emphatical Word; that is, emphatical either in its Sound or Senſe.

By this Art many a Writer conciliates to himſelf more Applauſe than he deſerves. And it's wonderful to think how ſtrong a Prepoſſeſſion, a neat and numrous Diction gives you in Favour of your Author. It often compenſates a Defect of Thought; and, like a muſical Interlude between the Acts, keeps you in good Humour till you meet with better Entertainment. At leaſt, it poliſhes and adorns a low Thought (as fine Clothes do an ordinary Perſon) in ſuch a Manner as to give you a better Opinion of it than is due to its intrinſick Worth. Hence ſome Writers have ſerved themſelves of this Art ſo far as to turn it into mere Artifice; and by Means of a ſweet and flowing Stile, adorned with here and there a vivid Phraſe and brilliant Expreſſion, have wrote themſelves into Fame without Thought; (for as one obſerves (*o*) *it's a much eaſier Matter to Write than to think*) whilſt the injudicious Reader takes all the Tinſel for true Sterling.

However if this Science be Subject to Abuſe (and what is not?) does it therefore deſerve Contempt? If Fools and Fops appear in rich and gay Attire, that is no Reaſon ſure that a Man of Senſe ſhould be a Sloven.

In

(*n*) Ex omnibus Metr's Sermoni quotidiano accommodatum maximè eſt *Iambicum*. Cui rei id Signo eſt quod plurima nos Iambica proferamus imprudentes in Collocutione mutua. *Poetic.* c. 2.

(*o*) *Fitzoſborn.* Let. lvii.

In a Word, it's sufficient Recommendation of this Subject, that *Longinus* himself makes it a Branch of the true Sublime; by Vertue of which many of the Antients acquired the Reputation of fine Writers, who had little else to entitle them to that Character. For sais he——" Several Poets and other Writers possessed of
" no natural Sublimity, or rather entire Strangers to
" it, have very frequently made Use of common and
" vulgar Terms, that have not the least Air of E-
" legance to recommend them, yet by musically
" disposing and artfully connecting such Terms, they
" clothe their Periods in a Kind of Pomp, and dex-
" troufly conceal their intrinfick Lowness (*p*)." And this was what gave *Euripides* all his Fame; who, in the Judgment of that discerning Critic, *excelled rather in fine Composition than in fine Sentiments* (*q*).

And that which was in so high Esteem among the Antients, I cannot but think, for the Reasons before mentioned, deserves a more particular Regard than it hath yet met with from the Moderns.

(*p*) *Longin.* de Sublim, Sect. xxxiv.
(*q*) Τῆς συνθέσεως ποιητὴς ὁ Εὐριπίδης μᾶλλόν ἐστιν, ἢ τοῦ νοῦ. *Ibid.*

F I N I S.

CPSIA information can be obtained
at www.ICGtesting.com
Printed in the USA
LVHW082134080419
613369LV00064B/1608/P